THE FINANCIAL ADVISOR FIELD GUIDE

What They Don't Teach at Financial Planning School

Robert Cucchiaro, CFP®

CONTENTS

INTRODUCTION

"Don't write to make money, write to build relationships with likeminded people that you haven't yet met." Naval Ravikant

This is the book I wish I had read 17+ years ago when I was first starting in the business. My goal here is not to say we've got it all figured out and that you should do things exactly as we have. In fact, there are a lot of ways to be successful in this business and in many ways, I've simply taken what I've seen other successful advisors doing and put my own spin on it. I've started the book with this quote from Naval precisely because I didn't write this book to make any money, I wrote it to pay it forward. My career has been boosted by the many mentors I've been fortunate to have. Now I hope to do the same and boost others in their careers.

Before we dive in, I want to share what initially attracted me to the career, something my now long-time business coach, friend and mentor said to me at our very first meeting 18+ years ago. It's called the 3 I's.

Nick Horn is a legend in our industry and might be right behind Ray Kroc in terms of the number of people he helped become millionaires.

At our first meeting in December of 2003 Nick told me that this profession was the only one he could think of that offered the "3 I's" as he called them – **Independence, Impact & Income**. We spent quite a bit of time just on this concept alone and Nick completely sold me on the fact that if I became an Advisor, I could have the independence to work whatever hours I wanted to and be a part of my kids' lives (I didn't have kids but I hoped someday I would I knew this would be important to me). He sold me on the idea that left to their own devices, people don't always make the best financial decisions. Given my personal background with my own parents, it was not hard for him to convince me of this. Plus, I knew that I would not be happy with any career unless it had a positive impact on others. And finally, he told me that if I worked hard and took advantage of whatever opportunities came my way, that I would make a very good living and build a business with real value.

My hope in writing this book is that I can do for others what Nick Horn once did for me.

Author's note - Throughout this book I mention templates that I've developed over the years that I am still using in practice today with my clients. All of these are available for download on our website:
https://thefinancialadvisorfieldguide.com

FOREWORD BY RYAN PRICE, CFP®, CHFC, CLU, CRPC, AWMA

Rob's been helping me think strategically about my business for the past 17 years, since we first started working together at Lincoln Financial back in 2005. One of the core themes of this book is that systems are better than *winging it* and Rob is all about having a system for everything. That's why for the past few years I've been encouraging him to write all of this down and share it with the rest of the Advisor community. His hesitation of course, is that the system is never finished. It is always being refined, there is always room for improvement.

I got into this business during my senior year in college. I had no background in finance, my degree was in business marketing, so while I knew breaking in would be difficult, I had no idea just how difficult. Like Rob, I've been blessed to have the same mentor in Nick Horn and the same training from Lincoln Financial, but that's where our stories diverged. Throughout the 10+ years we worked together at Lincoln, Rob was my manager, mentor, and friend. We still collaborate and share business goals and plans, discuss case design, do's and don'ts of planning, and share best practices anytime we discover a new technique or strategy.

For the past 5 years I've been complaining to him that there isn't a book to teach financial advisors how to be… financial advisors. There are plenty of books with content about financial advice. But there aren't books or resources that discuss the business aspect of financial services – "working *on* the business and not *in* the business" as we commonly say. There isn't a book about approach, systems, and the soft skills that it takes to be a successful advisor.

Furthermore, my experience as an adjunct professor teaching financial planning for the past decade, I've also observed this gap. My role here is to turn financial advisors into Certified Financial Planners™. Unfortunately, none of this content is being taught in any of the texts nor is it part of the CFP® curriculum. As such, there isn't a blueprint to teach someone, how to actually be an advisor. How does an advisor communicate with prospects and clients? How do they learn the soft skills, and how to be a good listener? How do they market and get new clients?

When I started in the business 20 years ago, I was taught marketing by trial and error: Cold call business owners out of the phone book. Meet a bunch of centers of influence and strategic alliances and try to form partnerships. Join networking groups. It was truly trial by fire and on the job training. I really wish that during my time studying for my CFP® that there was a course designed to teach the *art of the business*.

This book is designed to bridge that gap between what you learn technically and what you really <u>need</u> to know, to learn about financial services.

Hope you enjoy it and learn as much from it as I have over the course of my career.

ABOUT THE AUTHOR / MY QUALIFICATIONS

There's nothing worse than taking advice from a so called "expert" only to later find out that they are better at giving advice than they were at doing the thing they are opining about. I always laugh when I hear some industry guru talk about practice management only to find out they failed as an Advisor and had to pivot to telling Advisor's what they should be doing. To ensure that's not the case here, a little background on me. I entered the financial services industry right out of college (Cornell, class of 2002) and joined a large insurance company that also owned a large broker-dealer and had about 8,000 financial advisors. After spending 2 years in the home office, I knew I wanted to be a Financial Advisor, so I made my way into a field office in my 3rd year, before becoming an Advisor in my 4th year. By my 5th year in the industry, I was both an Advisor and a Regional Vice President where I managed 80 financial advisors. My first year as an Advisor was a success as I was lucky enough to find a mentor who gave me 100 names I could call, folks he had done business with at some point in his long career. By my 5th year as an FA, I was doing about $350K of revenue per year, at which point I left the insurance-owned broker-dealer and joined the wealth management firm I own today. Fast forward to today and I own and operate a 10-person wealth management firm. We manage over $700 million of client assets and work with 275 high net worth families. Our average recurring revenue per client is around $15,000.

I personally serve as the Primary Advisor for 115 of these families and spend 80% of my time as an Advisor and 20% of my time running the business.

Finally, a few quick things you should know about this book

1. There is no overlap with CFP® curriculum – the goal of this book is to teach you what I've seen and what I know (both the good and the bad). Nothing in here will overlap with what you've learned by going through the CFP® process. I think becoming a CFP® should be the minimum requirement for the profession, so my goal is not to compete or take away from that but rather to say, these are the lessons you can learn the hard way, or the easy way and I hope to make things easier for you as the reader.

2. This book was intended to serve more as a textbook than a novel. While I hope it is an interesting read from cover to cover, my goal is for you to be able to pick up this book when you run into a specific situation or question and get some perspective on how to handle things. As a result, the book has been written

in 4 distinct sections which follow what I call "The Wealth Management Model" – **See Figure 1**

3. The book then concludes with one section on 'running the business' followed by a few case studies and anecdotes from my career that I think you will find helpful.

Figure 1

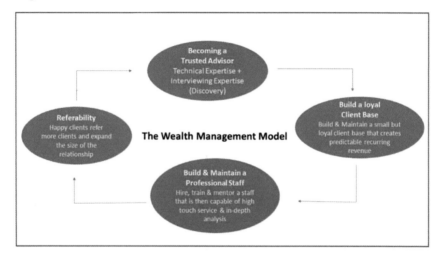

SECTION I

BECOMING A
TRUSTED ADVISOR

Before we dive into what it takes to become a Trusted Advisor, this book is designed for Advisors with 3+ years of experience. I say this because if you've made it 3 years you are likely going to make it. When I was hiring and training Advisors the national statistics were that 85% of new Advisors fail within the 1st 3 years. I haven't researched these stats lately and perhaps they've improved as newer Advisors now are usually hired into existing teams which certainly helps, but the fact remains, the 1st 3 years are the equivalent of Hell Week – survive those and you are on your way.

This book is also designed for the 1% of Advisors that truly want to be great and are willing to do what is necessary to get there. This career can be incredibly rewarding both spiritually and financially, but it doesn't come easy.

I was very fortunate to have mentors who coached me and helped me expedite my learning curve. But one thing I noticed early on was that my mentors developed their wisdom and expertise by simply being in the field for 20+ years and learning over time. **I was not willing to wait 20 years to become a great Advisor!** So instead, I took a different approach and it worked for me. I am now going to share some of these same "growth and learning hacks" with you.

Earning Someone's Trust

There are entire books you can read that will help you better understand what it takes to earn someone's trust. I would start with David Maister's *The Trusted Advisor* and Robert Cialdini's *Influence: The Psychology of Persuasion*. From my perspective, there are 3 things that are required to become a Trusted Advisor:

1. Develop technical expertise
2. Adopt a great discovery process & mindset
3. The ability to implement and execute

This section is centered on how one can obtain technical expertise quickly. But before we dive into the details, a quick preface:

Early in my career I remember an older Advisor (who wasn't very technically proficient) telling me that you could be the most technically sound Advisor in the world, and it wouldn't matter if you didn't get out there and market yourself. There is certainly some truth to that and it's one of the reasons I recommend you read the book *Selling the Invisible* (more on that later). At the same time, if you get in front of prospective clients and you lack the technical knowledge needed to help them make better financial decisions, your marketing efforts will fail as they will not result in prospective clients becoming actual clients.

How does one obtain Technical Expertise?

First and foremost, get your CFP® designation. **This is the #1 piece of advice I would give a new Advisor.**

Second, figure out what kind of clients you want to work with and what issues matter to those types of clients. For example, if you want to work with corporate executives you need to know as much as you can about RSUs (restricted stock units), options, employee stock purchase plans, 10b5-1 plans. Be sure when figuring this out, that you pick something you are genuinely interested in learning about. Otherwise, the learning process will be a grind. As I like to tell my kids, everything is easier if you are enjoying it. If you enjoy learning about taxes and tax strategies, then doing so isn't a chore or a homework assignment but rather something you love.

Finally, make a commitment to lifelong learning. Throughout this book I mention books you should read, podcasts you should listen to, blogs you should subscribe to, etc. If you are serious about the profession and want to build a $1M+ recurring revenue business, you must become the kind of Advisor successful families would want to hire. And that means a lifetime commitment to learning and staying current.

Let's now dive deep into exactly how I would recommend one goes about achieving technical expertise and where learning starts, after obtaining one's CFP® designation.

Developing Technical Expertise - Learning Comes before Earning

"Become so good that they can't ignore you" – Steve Martin

Early in my career, when I was just 25 years old, one of my mentors paid me a huge compliment that boosted my confidence and encouraged me to keep doing what I was doing. He said that even though I looked young, and clients knew I was young, as soon as I started talking, I demonstrated the fact that I knew what I was talking about and that gave clients the confidence needed to look past my age.

That was not by accident. A Trusted Financial Advisor is no different from a doctor or a lawyer in that, the advice we give matters and has a huge impact on other people's lives. We therefore owe it to them to "know our stuff" which also means we owe it to them to stay abreast of new developments, tax law changes, new strategies, new products, etc.

The hardest part about being new in any profession is the early period where you are still figuring things out and you aren't getting paid much for your work. Inevitably people want to shortcut this process, many simply because they can't live off what they are making. In my experience there is only one shortcut that works and it's becoming a technical expert.

I often tell new Advisors "you have to learn before you can earn". Some learning can be done from reading, other learning must be done through experience.

The two best ways to speed up this process are 1) **Read everything that the titans of our industry put out** and 2) **Get in front of as many people as possible.**

Reading/Podcasts/Webinars

This means that in addition to working 40-50 hours per week, you will be spending another 10-20 hours per week reading, listening to podcasts, and watching webinars.

Where will you find the time you ask? Let me give you an example; for the past 7 years my kids have trained in jiu jitsu for an hour a day, 3 to 4 days per week. Rather than drop them off and pick them up like most of the other parents, for 7 years I have sat there during class reading.

I know of another great Advisor who spends 5-6 hours a week in his car, commuting to the office, going to see clients, etc. He spends that entire time listening to industry related podcasts.

If it's important enough to you, you will find the time.

Not all reading is treated equally. I would suggest that reading Baron's or Forbes or anything like that might seem important but will not give you the edge you need to turbocharge your career. Here are the things I encourage you to read to thrive and be successful:

- Everything that **Michael Kitces** puts out. This means the Nerd's Eye View blog plus all of his industry articles.
- Everything that **Ed Slott** puts out. This includes the paid subscription for his monthly newsletter plus all of his industry articles.
- Everything that **Nick Murray** puts out. This includes the paid subscription for his monthly newsletter (Nick Murray Interactive) + all of his books. Some of his books are $100 or more and guess what, they are more than worth it!
- **The Kiplinger Tax Newsletter** – this is a 4 pager that comes out every 2 weeks and is well worth the cost.
- **Financial Advisor Magazine** – this is free for financial advisors and this monthly magazine never disappoints.
- **Martin Shenkman** – author of several books (all worth reading) and regular webinar host. Read his books, listen to his webinars, sign up for his newsletter.
- **Ross Levin** – Industry legend, author of The Wealth Management Index (which you should not only read but read annually), Ross is still a practicing Advisor with a thriving business. He writes for the Minnesota Tribune, and I have a google alert set so that anytime he writes anything I am made aware of it.

To that end, you should start building your library. Here is where a Great Financial Advisor would start:

- *Implementing the Wealth Management Index* by Ross Levin
- *The New Financial Advisor* by Nick Murray
- *Basic Truths for Financial Life Planners - Building a Profitable Client-Centered Practice* by Roy Dilberto
- *The Overtaxed Investor: Slash Your Tax Bill & Be a Tax Alpha Dog* by Phil Demuth
- *The New Advisor for Life* by Stephen Gresham
- *The Estate Planner's Tool Book* by Paul Hood & Edwin Morrow
- *Smart Portfolios* by Robert Carver
- *Retire Secure* by James Lange
- *Selling the Invisible* by Harry Beckwith
- *The Top 40 Tax Planning Opportunities for 2022* (updated annually) by Robert Keebler & Peter Melcher
- *Global Asset Allocation* by Meb Faber
- *Your Money Ratios* by Charles Farrell
- *Paychecks and Playchecks* by Tom Hegna
- *The Millionaire Next Door* by Thomas Stanley

There are 14 books on this list – read one a month and in just over a year you will know more about Financial Planning than 90% of your competition.

Podcasts

Just like you should fill your downtime with reading, you should fill your drive time or your gym time with podcasts. Here are some of my favorites:

- **Financial Advisor Success Podcast** with Michael Kitces
- **The Meb Faber Show**
- **Capital Allocators** with Ted Seides
- **Invest like the Best** with Patrick O' Shaughnessy
- **Gestalt University** by Resolve Asset Management
- **Between Now and Success** with Steve Sanduski
- **RIA Edge** with Mark Bruno
- **Trillions** – an ETF podcast

Webinars

Round out your knowledge and tackle some more advanced topics with webinars, especially around subjects where visuals can aid in your learning. Here are some of my favorites:

- **Leimberg Information Services** – if it's tax planning and/or estate planning, these guys are the best. You have to pay for their webinars but they include handouts and you can listen to them more than once.
- **CPA Academy** – they have weekly webinars, some for free, others you have to pay for the content.
- **Jackson National** – always free and these range from mutual fund portfolio managers to retirement income planning strategies.

- **Shenkman Law** – Martin Shenkman is a wealth of information and a gift to our entire profession. He and his partners from InterActive Legal offer free webinars at least monthly and often more frequently than that.

This may seem overwhelming but if you expect clients to take you seriously, pay for and act on your advice and recommendations, <u>you have to become an expert</u>. And if you want to earn $1,000,000 per year in this business, your expertise has to extend beyond "spend less than you earn, buy index funds and get some term insurance."

When I meet with a prospective client I tell them at the first meeting what our fee structure is and if they've never worked with an Advisor before, they will often ask "what do I get for $10,000?" (as an example). Because I am an expert I can quickly rattle off a few examples of areas where I can improve their situation and the value of our recommendation is a multiple of my fee. This expertise comes from the time and dedication that has been put in over the years.

Resources for Financial Advisors

Our industry is overflowing with helpful resources, and it is our job to maximize them for our client's benefit. I think one of the things that makes our industry so unique is our willingness to share best practices with one another.

Here is a partial list of resources I use to run my business:

Resource	Practice Area	Free or Paid
Portfolio Visualizer	Investment Management	Free
Cambria Investments / Investing Insights	Investment Management	Free
Nick Murray Interactive	Investments & Retirement	Paid
Leimberg Information Services	Estate Planning & Tax Planning	Paid
Keebler Monthly Bulletin	Estate Planning & Tax Planning	Paid
Kitces.com Member Section	All things financial planning	Paid
JP Morgan Guide to the Markets	Investments & Economic Updates	Free
Bradford Tax Institute	Tax Strategy	Paid
Koyfin	Capital Markets	Free
Local FPA Chapter Meetings	All things financial planning	Paid
Wholesalers	Product specific	Free
Relationship Managers at your Custodian	Practice Management	Free

If all of this seems overwhelming or beyond your monthly budget, form a best practices group with a few other like-minded Advisors and divide and conquer some of these.

One more thing – consider these costs the financial planner's equivalent of "COGS – cost of goods sold". In non-service businesses, a business owner buys something for a $1 and turns around and sells it for $1.50, hoping to net a profit after operating expenses. The $1 they spent on the item is their cost of goods sold. We don't have that in our profession. Our cost of goods sold is the time we spend trying to become good enough that someone will want to hire us; the time we spend trying to find good clients, and the money we spend on education so we can become experts.

Getting Real Life Experience

Now let's talk about "getting some at bats" – any meeting with a client or a prospective client is an at bat. Practice makes perfect and the more client/prospect meetings you sit in, the more practice you are getting. If you are at a firm with 50 clients in total and those clients come in once a year, it's going to take you a long time to get enough at bats to become an expert. My advice for new professionals who are coming into the industry is to pick the opportunity that will give you the most at bats, regardless of the pay structure. In the first 3-5 years in the business, you won't make much money no matter where you are (Wirehouse, RIA, family office, bank, etc.) so you might as well view that time the way a doctor views going to medical school. The goal is to get a ton of varied experience, where in one meeting you are talking about real estate, the next active vs. passive investments, and the next advance estate planning. You will need several good mentors who are willing to sit in meetings with you, or even better, let you sit in meetings with them.

Later on, we will talk about how to structure your week but for now let me just say that the perfect week features a combination of learning and "at bats".

Adopting a Great Discovery Process & Mindset

We've all heard of or even experienced great doctors or surgeons that have a terrible bed side manner. In our profession the equivalent would be someone who is technically proficient but who lacks the empathy and listening skills necessary to really make a difference in a client's life. For example, if early in the on-boarding process a client tells you that their biggest fear is running out of money, three meetings later when you suggest they make a large irrevocable gift to charity, their kids, grandkids, etc. don't be surprised when you get pushback and an unwillingness to move forward. That doesn't mean that your strategy isn't technically sound, it just means you didn't hear the person the way you needed to.

If you've never heard of the phrase "discovery", it's simply the process that you go through with a prospective client at the beginning of the relationship where you take both qualitative and quantitative information. The quantitative part is easy, net worth, investments, taxes, etc. Any CFP® Practitioner knows exactly what this means. But what about the qualitative part?

Our Discovery Process is as follows:

1. The 1st stage in the process varies slightly between 'leads' vs. referrals. A 'lead' has no existing connection

to our firm (maybe they found us via Google search) whereas a referral found us from either an existing client or an existing COI (CPA, attorney, etc.). With a 'lead' we do a bit of screening on the front end to make sure we aren't wasting each other's time before the meeting is even conducted. We are less concerned about this with a referral as we feel that we owe it to the person who made the referral to at least take the meeting even if we are not the right fit for the prospective client.

2. We send an email confirming our meeting and in it we include an attachment called "The Financial Life Checkup." This is a one-page questionnaire that simply asks the person how they feel about their existing planning on a scale of 1 to 5. Everything from "how satisfied are you with your existing investment strategy" to "how comfortable are you with the amount of insurance you carry?". If we are dealing with two spouses, we will ask that each complete this questionnaire separately.

3. In this same email we will ask the prospective client to either bring to the meeting or send in advance 2 things

    a. Their most recent tax returns – all pages
    b. Their investment account statements

In that same email I will say "if for whatever reason you are pressed for time and can only bring one thing to the meeting, please bring your tax returns. And if you want, you can simply email your CPA and copy me and ask him/her to send them to us so we can review them in advance."

Early in my career I would send prospective clients a "document checklist" asking them for everything from their tax returns to their life insurance policies to their mortgage statement. Ultimately I will need all of this if the person decides to hire us – but I don't need it for the initial meeting and asking for it created a 'homework assignment' for the prospect that actually delayed the process getting started.

4. At that first meeting we will conduct discovery by using an intake form. We use a 2-page intake form where page 1 is all qualitative and page 2 is all quantitative. Our **intake form** can be downloaded from the website and as you will see, includes questions like where did you grow up, what did you study in school, did you grow up with money, are you providing financial support for any family members and/or do you expect to in the future. These questions are intended to open up the dialogue and let you really learn about the person before you make recommend-dations to them. (This background is also the first building block to creating a strong client relationship.)

   a. One interesting thing I've learned over the years is that when I send out the intake form in advance, people tend to go deeper when answering the qualitative questions.

5. At that first meeting I always use an agenda, which is as follows:

    a. **Initial Call/Concerns**
    b. **Complete Template for Data Discovery**
    c. **Review Financial Life Check-up**
    d. **Discuss Summit Wealth & Retirement and our Services Offered**
    e. **Review Holistiplan Sample Scenario Comparison**
    f. **Quote fee – complete Wealth Management**
    g. **Proposal**
    h. **Next Steps**

We also have a similar intake form when it comes to investments (questions like what is the best investment you've ever made and why?) and another intake form for estate planning which asks about charitable intents, separate property, and things of that nature.

When it comes to the Discovery Process, Financial Advisors can learn more from folks like Charlie Rose and believe it or not, Howard Stern, than they can learn from the talking heads on CNBC. The reason I say this is because Charlie Rose and Howard Stern are masters at getting the person sitting across the table from them to open up. And if you want to have deep, meaningful, long-lasting relationships with your clients, you must do the same.

Well Actually...

I mentioned earlier that when I was young, I was able to overcome my youth being an obstacle because I was technically proficient. The downside of this was that when I was talking to a prospective client and they said something that was technically incorrect, I wouldn't hesitate to correct them.

I was very fortunate in that one day I was seeing a prospective client with one of my mentors and trainers, Aaron Jeung, when I decided to correct the person sitting across the table from us. In the car ride back to the office Aaron said, "don't argue with people if you want them to hire you", to which I argued "but what she said was factually incorrect." Aaron taught me that day how to reframe without arguing.

Let me give you some real-life examples I've encountered:

Client – "Annuities are terrible investments because they are a waste of money."

My response – "I can see why you would say that as most people's perception of annuities is just that. And the media hasn't helped much with folks like Suzie Orman and Ken Fisher villainizing those products. But let me ask you a question – do you know anyone that receives monthly income from an annuity? Because I know a lot of people that do, including both of my parents, and I must say having that guaranteed check each month on top of their Social Security helps them sleep better at night and makes them less worried about the stock market".

From there I would ask their permission to share some educational materials with them about annuities in general and see if they were willing to learn a bit more before closing the door on these products. I've found most of the time the person was willing to go down that path with me.

Client – "I would never pay for a financial plan when I could just get one for free from my life insurance guy."

My response – "That makes sense. The only thing you might want to ask yourself is why is your life insurance guy spending 15-20 hours analyzing your entire financial situation for free. And the answer is either 1) he isn't, he's spending an hour or so doing high level calculations which isn't a real financial plan, or 2) he's doing just enough planning to figure out how much insurance you need, so he can sell you that insurance. Now to be clear, there is nothing wrong with selling insurance, we sell insurance too and each year it makes up between 1% and 5% of our revenue. But we sell insurance as part of an overall financial plan, we don't do planning in order to sell insurance. The reason someone would pay a flat fee for a financial plan is because they want objectivity. I think given your financial situation and the complexity you are dealing with; you could see a very good return on your investment by hiring an independent Advisor. But if you are not interested, I understand."

Nothing works all of the time, including these reframing statements. But I've found that people are much more open minded and willing to hear me out after I agree with whatever they just said. Starting my rebuttals with "Well actually" gets me nowhere.

Implement the Ability to Execute - Making Good on Your Promises

Later in the book we talk about how to make sure you and your team can deliver on your promises but for now, let me just state the following – to become a Trusted Advisor one must make good on their promises. Too many people still view the Financial Advisor profession as a sales profession instead of an advice profession. All of the things that we discuss in this book will ultimately help with changing that perception. **But the one thing that everyone hates about "salespeople" is that they make empty promises.** The ability to execute means the ability to deliver on the promises you make during the prospective client phase where you successfully convince a new client to hire you and your firm. For example, if you say "we run mock tax returns for our clients each and every year to see if there is anything different they should be doing at year-end" you better have a process in place to make good on that statement.

The System is the Solution

My mentor and business coach likes to say, "if you have a problem, create a system and soon you will no longer have a problem." One of the themes throughout my career has been to conduct a post-mortem after a problem arises or a crisis occurs and try to figure out what can be done proactively to prevent this from happening again.

That same business coach and friend likes to say, "you must inspect what you expect". It's not enough to create a system, you also must periodically test it to make sure it still works. Human nature is that once we put a system into place, we tend to forget about it and assume it's working as planned.

To combat that remember the following - C.R.I.S. which stands for Crisis / Response / Improvement / Complacency.

Sometimes you will hear someone say (sarcastically) "it worked so well that we stopped doing it." If you want to build a sustainable business, you have to not only build the systems but test them and make sure they are still being used.

Wrapping Up

When I take on a new client, I am making a commitment to them and to their family that I will help them with everything in their life that has a dollar sign attached to it, and some other things that do not. Furthermore, I tell my clients that my job is simply to help them make better financial decisions. It's not just to run projections or manage portfolios. Finally, I tell them that I take personal responsibility for seeing that their plan gets designed, implemented, and monitored and that I will proactively reach out to them when it's time to make a change.

To honor these commitments, I must have systems in place (and a great team that supports me).

If you want clients to see you as a Trusted Advisor, worthy of managing their wealth, you must constantly prove to them that you are a consummate professional. Once a promise to a client has been made, if not kept, all future promises lose

credibility. And I need not remind you what happens in a relationship once credibility is gone.

SECTION II

BUILDING A LOYAL CLIENT BASE

To build up your client base, you must be able to do two things effectively:

1. Get in front of potential clients
2. Convince the potential clients you get in front of that you are worthy of being hired

In our next series we will devote considerable time to getting in front of potential clients. For now, because I am assuming the readers of this book have 3 years or more of experience, hopefully by now you are using some marketing techniques and are not starting from scratch.

To that end, below are some thoughts on both subjects.

Obtaining Clients & Marketing

"Help enough people get what they want and eventually you will get what you want" – Zig Zigler

The old joke in this business is that when you're new and someone asks, "who do you work with" you might say something like "business owners" or "retirees" but your real answer is "anyone that can fog a mirror". Trust me I remember those days and truth be told, I'm glad I didn't form a niche too early in my career because when I look at my client base today, clients' range in age, profession, net worth, and just about every other category.

The first thing you will need to think about is **who you are going to work with**. Because this single decision will dictate how you market, what you read, where you focus your expertise, and who ends up on your team.

Let me give you some examples:

> **Business Owners** - Your marketing plan might be to partner with a CPA firm that works with business owners, or to partner with an HR consultant that advises businesses that are too small to have a full time HR person on staff. Your expertise might be around setting up retirement plans (401K, profit sharing plans, cash balance pension plans, etc.). You will need to become an expert in key man life insurance, key man disability, and cross purchase business succession planning. You will need to understand how LLCs and S Corps are formed, how they are taxed, and how to read their financials. Your network will consist of business attorneys, health insurance consultants, HR consultants, commercial RE

brokers and pretty much any professional that serves this same target market.

Executives with Stock Options/RSUs - Your marketing plan might be to cold email executives from one particular business and try to get just a couple of clients at this company who can then refer you to their co-workers. Your expertise needs to be around all of the benefits that these executives have access to, which might include the company 401K plan, the company stock purchase plan, RSUs, options, and maybe even deferred compensation or a pension plan. You will need to understand this company's particular stock and things like zero-cost collars, pre-paid forward sales, and charitable remainder trusts.

Retirees – Your marketing plan might be to host seminars on Social Security or public pensions (PERS, CALSTRS, etc.) Your expertise needs to be around all things related to retirement which will include strategies for taking Social Security, pension maximization, annuities, safe withdrawal rates, tax projections, etc. You will need to build a network that can help address questions retirees might have about things like Medicare, reverse mortgages, moving out of State for tax purposes, funding grandchildren's 529 plans and a host of others.

You cannot be all things to all people. And while financial planning at its core shares more similarities than differences (spend less than you earn, invest the difference, diversify, protect with insurance, etc.) as you move up the financial planning pyramid you need to develop expertise in specific areas. At our firm we have chosen to work with Retirees and Real Estate Investors as our primary client types and we've developed expertise in all things related to these client-types. We have a few business owner clients which we can handle because we are business owners ourselves and simply advise clients to do many of the same strategies we are doing ourselves. However, we do not work with executives with stock options by choice and when we receive incoming inquiries from these folks, we advise them that we are not the right fit.

The Purpose of Your Mission Statement

Before our firm had a Mission Statement, I assumed Mission Statements were for large bureaucratic organizations and were just fluff. I believe strongly in substance over form, so the appeal of a Mission Statement was lost on me. But let me tell you, this is no longer the case and here's why.

If you work with a team, you need everyone to be on the same page. Part of being on the same page means coming to an agreement about who you want to work with. Our Mission Statement says:

> *The primary mission of Summit Wealth & Retirement Partners (SWRP) is to help successful people <u>make better financial decisions</u> and <u>feel more secure about their money</u>.*

We accomplish our mission by providing highly customized financial advice, and always putting our client's best interest above all else.

We deliver on our promise by having well defined roles and responsibilities, utilizing a consistent methodology for analyzing client data, presenting our observations & recommendations in a clear manner, and keeping detailed notes of our actions.

Our job is to help clients by <u>designing</u>, <u>implementing</u>, and <u>monitoring</u> their customized financial plans.

As a firm, our strengths include our <u>servant mentality</u>, our <u>commitment to high quality</u> at all times, and our <u>dedication to lifelong learning</u>.

We are especially suited to help those with complex needs who believe in outsourcing their most pressing financial decisions to a Trusted Advisor.

While I could go through the importance of each of these individual statements, there are 3 that I would like to emphasize and share how they help get everyone on the same page.

- *The primary mission of Summit Wealth & Retirement Partners (SWRP) is to help successful people <u>make better financial decisions</u> and <u>feel more secure about their money</u>.* Hopefully this goes without saying, but it's imperative that we all understand what we are being hired to do and that clients agree. Notice this doesn't say our mission is just to build a certain type of portfolio or just to design a certain kind of tax strategy.

- *Our job is to help clients by designing, implementing, and monitoring their customized financial plans.* We want our clients and our team to know that they are hiring us to perform 3 separate and distinct tasks, which cannot be untangled from one another. This way if a client says they want to hire us to do design only (we create the plan, they implement themselves at Vanguard or with term insurance and then they occasionally hire us to monitor) we can firmly state that no, we are not interested in that kind of work. When you have multiple Advisors on the team this steadfastness around a common mission is extremely important because otherwise Advisor A may agree to this type of 'design only' planning while the other Advisors disagree and that is bad for the business in numerous ways.
- *We are especially suited to help those with complex needs who believe in outsourcing their most pressing financial decisions to a Trusted Advisor.* – Out of all of the subcomponents of our Mission Statement, **this one is the most important.** When one of the Advisors on the team tells me that they are struggling with whether or not to bring on some prospective new client that they met with, I will always start by asking "does this person have complex financial needs and believe in outsourcing their financial decision making to a Trusted Advisor?" If the answer is yes, then the discussion can continue. Because our firm's growth has included what

I will call two mini-acquisitions, this same litmus test is applied to existing clients who we occasionally will have to part ways with when we realize (or accept) the fact that they don't really believe in outsourcing their financial decision making to a Trusted Advisor.

All Forms of Marketing & What Worked for Me

"Honest Intelligent Effort is Always Rewarded…. Eventually."

The hardest part about marketing is that different things work for different people/firms and different strategies work differently over time. For example, when I was first starting in the business in 2005, believe it or not, everyone had a home phone. My firm's marketing plan was to call someone else's "old leads" – not an uncommon strategy for young Advisors when they get hired at an insurance-based firms or a brokerage firm.

These kinds of firms usually have a list of customers who at one point purchased a product (brokerage account, 529, life insurance policy) but no longer have an active relationship with an Advisor. This is actually how I got started in the business when one of my mentors gave me a list of 100 people that he had enrolled into a 403b plan at some point in his career. The good news about these folks is that you are not exactly cold calling them and can use their existing product/account as a valid reason for contacting them. The bad news is that, often times no one has a valid phone number or even better, an email address for these folks. In addition, calls to these customers often lead to service questions about their existing product which pays you nothing to handle.

Today there are many forms of marketing for Financial Advisors that either didn't exist or barely existed when I first started and they include things like paying for leads, hosting webinars, and targeting professionals via LinkedIn.

For more on this topic – go to Kitces.com/264 and listen to Michael's interview with Dan Callahan about all things related to Outsourcing Lead Generation.

My take on all of these is as follows:

1. You must pick something that works for you based on who you are. I tried hosting seminars and was **not** successful with it. Apparently I am not a great public speaker and I tend to do better one on one vs. in a large crowd.

2. You must pick something you enjoy or else you will not stick with it and if you do not stick with it, it will not work. Success comes with consistent effort, especially with something like this. You can hire a marketing consultant to tell you how easy it will be because their system is so great but at the end of the day, getting a stranger to hand you large sums of money to invest has never been easy and requires a lot of trust, which takes time.

Other forms of marketing that have also worked for me include:

Centers of Influence – this means getting in front of the other Advisors in your clients or prospective client's lives. Quite candidly, this one has been a mix bag for me. Some Advisors who I have great relationships with and whom I share many clients with never refer anyone to me whereas others I barely know or share just one client with have sent me tons of referrals.

Buying a Practice – In my career I've bought clients from two different Advisors. When I joined my current firm, it was under the guise that I would take over and buy out the existing owner, which I did after a two year gestation period. With that purchase I acquired approximately forty clients, 95% of which I still serve today. Then in 2017 through my relationship manager at Charles Schwab Institutional I met a local Advisor who wanted to take the 1st step towards retirement by selling me twenty of his clients. In both cases what made these opportunities work was that: 1) I didn't overpay for the clients and 2) the clients were seeking the same type of services and relationship that I was seeking to offer. and 3) we didn't bite off more than we could chew. I've had multiple opportunities to buy businesses that were either larger or more complex than mine and I passed every time because I refuse to sacrifice our deliverables to existing clients in order to take on more clients than we can reasonably handle at one time.

Getting Referrals – by far the form of marketing that has worked best for me has been simply to get referrals from existing clients. I've tried the approach of asking for referrals and even attended a multi-day workshop on how to ask for referrals. This approach did not work for me though I'm sure it works for others. I would say the things that have worked for me and the reason I get 25-40 referrals each year is the following:

- Be referrable – promises made, promises kept
- Build genuine relationships with your clients without pretense
- Deserve them by providing great advice and being a positive influence in your client's lives
- Help your clients' other family members with no expectations (elderly parents, kids of any age)
- Let clients know you are still taking on new clients

Deserving and getting referrals is such an important topic that you will read more about this throughout the book.

Setting Asset Minimums

Throughout my career the question I struggled with the most was never technical in nature. It was always "what is your account minimum". I don't know why this was so hard for me to answer, but I guess it's because the honest answer is "it depends". Then one day several years ago when we were rebuilding our website, I dedicated some time to really thinking about this question. And the answer that I came up with has helped me ever since.

Our asset minimum varies based on the age of the client.

If a client is in their 30s and 40s, making good money and perhaps for the first time in their lives in a good position to save and invest, our asset minimum is only $500K (exceptions apply for the <u>adult children</u> of existing clients).

If a client is in their 50s to early 60s, our asset minimum is $1M. This is because we feel that $1M indicates that this person takes their financial future seriously enough that they've done something thus far and this person has enough assets to generate the revenue we need to justify the work we will do.

Finally, if a client is in their 70s or older, our account minimum is $2M (exceptions apply for the <u>parents</u> of existing clients). We are not miracle workers and, in our market, $2M is the minimum one would need to fulfill their financial wishes and obligations.

I've been using this methodology for several years now and I've found it's easier for prospective clients to understand.

As a follow up, here's what to do when you receive a referral from an existing client or COI and they **don't meet your minimum**.

"Dear Mrs. X,

I've now had a chance to review the financial information that you shared with me at our meeting on (Tuesday). Based on my review, I am going to suggest that you not hire us to manage your financial affairs and instead, reach out to a local Advisor that charges by the hour for financial planning services (these individuals can be found at www.napfa.org).

I came to this conclusion for a very simple reason – our minimum annual fee is ($5,000) and I cannot in good conscience charge you that for your financial planning needs, based on your situation. While I very much would like to help you, as a fiduciary I am compelled to make it clear to someone when my services are not suited to their needs.

I very much enjoyed meeting with you and will shred all personal/confidential information that you shared with me.

Sincerely,

Robert Cucchiaro, CFP®"

Building a Network

The purpose of your network is to benefit your clients, not to get referrals.

The best example of this that I can give is that my network includes some prominent criminal defense attorneys. I've had to lean on that network on more than one occasion when one of my client's sons got into legal trouble. I can assure you that I am not seeking referrals from these criminal defense attorneys, but I want them in my network because it benefits my clients in their time of need.

Traditionally, most financial advisors think of their network as CPAs and Attorneys. Needless to say, this is just the start, and a true network must extend far beyond these two types of professionals.

My network has been built over the past 17+ years entirely for the benefit of my clients. My goal is to make my client's lives easier and part of the way I accomplish that is by providing them access to professionals that I have screened & vetted. Now let me be clear on what this means – screened and vetted means I have personally worked with these folks and had a good experience. It doesn't mean they took me to lunch and presented well. I am only interested in referring my clients to other Advisors that are like-minded when it comes to responsiveness, creativity, organization, and client service.

At this point there are too many professionals in my network to name but here are just a few so you get the idea:

- CPA
- Estate Planning Attorney
- Business Attorney
- Tax Attorney
- Real Estate Attorney
- Executive Headhunter
- Business Broker
- Residential RE Mortgage Broker
- Commercial RE Mortgage Broker
- Commercial RE Broker
- Residential RE Agent

- Medicare Expert (out-sourced), we in-source Social Security expertise
- Philanthropic Expert (setting up Private Foundations)
- 1031 Exchange Expert

If you are doing this correctly, your network is constantly expanding. Every time I take on a new client there are potentially several new people in that client's life for me to consider adding to my network. Because my clients know how robust my network is, they come to me with problems that are often outside of the scope of traditional financial planning, knowing that I will have a resource that can help them. Without question, this deepens and strengthens our relationship and leads to greater loyalty.

Getting Compensated for Your Expertise

A lot of ink has been spilt on the fees involved in hiring a financial advisor. Unfortunately, a lot of that ink has been spilt by those in the industry who seem to have doubt over the value of the work they do. Perhaps it is because of our deep technical expertise and because of the quality of my team that this is not something I struggle with.

I've helped clients avoid bad decisions that would have cost them 20 times the fees they are paying me each year. I've talked clients down from the ledge when they wanted to panic and sell all their investments at the exact wrong time. I've helped clients keep their separate property separate only to later get divorced and be quite thankful that they did.

With that, here is how I've handled fees for my clients:

- We charge two separate fees for our work: 1) a flat fee for financial planning and 2) an assets under management (AUM) fee for direct asset management. I say direct because we don't charge on 401K plans or 529 plans if we are not the Advisor.
- Our flat fee ranges from $2,500 to $25,000.
- Our AUM fees start at 1% and decline as the client's assets with us exceed $2M.

We put our clients into 3 categories:

- HENRYs (high earners, not rich yet)
- Retirees or Near Retirees
- Wealth Management Clients

HENRYs are usually less than 55 years old, typically earn more than $400,000 per year, and have lots of moving parts in their financial lives. We charge these clients an annual planning fee on the lower end ($2,500-$3,500) plus our normal AUM fees.

Retirees or Near Retirees are usually over age 55 and have hired us because they have a single financial goal that drives everything, and it's a comfortable worry-free retirement. We charge these clients a one-time planning fee towards the middle of our range ($3,500-$5,500) plus our normal AUM fees. We do not work with these folks unless we are managing the bulk of their investment portfolio. Contrast this with HENRYs who often have

401K plans at work that we can advise on but don't charge for.

Wealth Management Clients are clients with a net worth over $10M who also have many moving parts in their lives. We charge these clients an annual planning fee on the higher end ($10K+) plus our normal AUM fees. For most of these clients the planning discussion goes from "do I have enough" to "how can I move money to my kids and grandkids in the most tax efficient way" or "how can I gift money without losing control" or "how can I give more to charity and should I set up a private foundation".

A few more comments & thoughts about fees:

1. **You can't compare what you charge to $0.** This may seem obvious, but I see FAs doing this all the time. Clients can hire you, hire the competition, or do it themselves. If a client wants to do it themselves, whatever fee you charge is too high. Your fees should be in line with your competitors, and you should be comparing yourself to firms that do what you do. So, if you are providing wealth management services to high-net-worth families, you shouldn't be comparing your fee structure to what Edward Jones is charging.

   a. All RIAs must publish their fee schedule annually in their ADV. At least once a year we pull our competitors' fee schedules and have them available to show prospective and existing clients. We want our clients to know that our fees are in line with our competitors. That is usually enough to put the fee discussion to rest.

2. **The fees are consistent but the value you create can be very lumpy.** With every client there will come a time where you will force them to do something that in retrospect, saved them a multitude of your fee. Sometimes it is forcing a client to get a pre-nup or to collar a concentrated stock position. Some piece of advice (put into action) as a safeguard against disaster. And when that disaster unfolds, the advice you gave saved them 10X your fee.

3. **Your fee schedule must line up with the type of business you want and the type of life you want.** When I was in management at my last firm, each Advisor worked with 700 families, on average. My firm has 4 full-time Advisors and combined we work with less than 300 families. Obviously those are two totally different business models. The typical Advisor at my last firm did about $350K of annual revenue. With 700 families that means each client was paying about $500 in annual revenue for the advice they were receiving. Today our firm does over $4M in revenue, which equates to $15K per family per year. My point here is not to say that my old firm did it wrong and we are doing it right, but rather to say there are different ways to build your firm and to think about fees. I'd rather have 70 clients with $5M each than 700 clients

with $500K each, but both work and both could produce the exact same revenue. However, the staffing models would be different and the expertise expected from the FA would be different.

4. **Stick to your guns** – when you are early in your career you may feel bashful about charging $5K to someone for your advice or $10K per year to manage someone's $1M portfolio. That is totally normal and just means you haven't been around long enough to see the value you will truly create for your clients. Feeling this is ok, acting on it is not. Once you come up with a fee schedule, stick with it and don't discount. I've had clients and prospective clients come up with all sorts of reasons why they should get a discount, or I should just charge them by the hour for my time instead. I'm proud to say my answer has consistently been "no" and as a result, it's rare that fees even come up anymore. But when they do, I simply compare our fees to our competitors fees and remind them of some of the many things I've helped them with over the years. On the other side, I've seen Advisors "make exceptions" to their fee schedule under the guise that after they do all this great work the client will then be willing to endure a fee increase. Sometimes that works but more than often, it doesn't.

5. List your fees on your website. If you go to my firm's website (https://summitwealthandretirement.com/) you will see that one of the main pages is titled "Our

Typical Clients/Pricing" and in that section we spell out the typical fee structure for various client engagements. When a prospective new client reaches out, I will ask them "have you visited our website" and if they say yes, I know they already have some sense for what we charge so there will be no surprises. If they say no, I send them the link and ask that they check it out before we meet. This step alone has led some "tire-kickers" to cancel their initial appointment with us and that's fine. I don't want to waste my time or theirs.

How to Talk About (or Defend) AUM Fees

- The key here is to pick a methodology that works for you and stick with it.
- For some that's as simple as saying "based on our fee structure, we do better when you and your investments do better".
- For others (engineers, CFAs, etc.) you will want to quantitatively justify this fee. Read about things like the Rebalancing Premium (which can be anywhere from 0.65% to over 2% per year) and have your "Why 1% (or whatever you charge) presentation ready to go. I know from personal experience that rebalancing alone can add over 1% in performance to client's accounts. I also know that without me, they would likely do lots of things that would impede their ability to meet their goals. Some would even invest in speculative disasters and lose lots of money.

I feel zero ambiguity about the value of my work in exchange for our fees, but I am biased by years of experience and witnessing firsthand some of the decision making that occurs, absent someone having a Trusted Advisor in their life.

Managing Client Relationships

Client Conversations

All conversations/meetings begin with a personal update. Money is a means to an end, and you can never forget that. If a client isn't sleeping well at night because they are worried about something, their rate of return for the previous quarter isn't worth mentioning. I must admit this was not something I understood early in my career (pre-kids especially). I thought all meetings should be mostly about business and often I missed cues that clients were bringing up that should have alerted me to the fact that something else was on their mind.

From there, the agenda is really dictated by the client type (HENRY vs. Retiree vs. Wealth Management Client) and the frequency of the meeting. For example, I meet with retirees or near retirees twice a year on average. The first meeting agenda consists of the following topics:

1. Personal Update
2. Actions Taken since previous meeting
3. Cash Flow & Balance Sheet Review

4. Retirement Projections
5. Portfolio Update
6. Next Steps

This meeting takes place between January and May of each year.

Then in the second meeting of the year the agenda looks like this:

1. Personal Update
2. Actions Taken since previous meeting
3. Cash Flow & Balance Sheet Review
4. Tax Projections
5. Portfolio Update
6. Next Steps

You will notice that the only major difference is that retirement projections are substituted for tax projections. This is for two reasons:

1. I don't believe in running retirement projections more than annually, and
2. I like to show clients what we expect their tax returns will look like come next April, and whether there is anything we can or should do before year-end to improve upon them.

   Recently I had a client who was near retirement and when we were doing his tax projections, he mentioned that his employer (law firm partnership) was buying back his stock before year-end. We ran two mock tax scenarios to show him that given his high earned income in the current year vs. his reduced earned income in his first year of retirement, convincing his firm to delay the stock purchase to the following year would save him about $10K in taxes. Unfortunately for him he was unable to convince his law partners to do this. But I know for certain that he now understands the importance of us running mock tax projections before the end of the year.

Regardless of how you like to structure your client review meetings, I suggest you include the following:

Agenda by Client Type / Top 3 most important things

HENRYs

- Savings % / Net worth relative to where it should be (based on age/income)
- Taking advantage of time horizon - Investing in Equities
- Reducing the tax bill

Retirees

- Withdrawal Rate %
- Asset allocation (draw down risk)
- Reducing the tax bill

Ultra-High Net Worth

- Portfolio Review
- Estate Plan & Tax Considerations – gifting and other techniques
- Reducing the tax bill

Presenting to Different Client Personalities

While our meeting agendas are very similar, the way we present things to clients varies greatly on their personality type. Running a business with support staff means you must have some level of consistency or else you are always reinventing the wheel. On the other hand, if you want to work with a small number of affluent clients, you need to customize what you are presenting based on who you are presenting to.

For example, I have two clients that are sisters and while they are similar in age and net worth, they are completely different in their style and decision making. One of the sisters wants every detail and any omission of facts is not looked kindly upon. Her sister on the other hand is very high level and believes in outsourcing decisions to the experts around her. For her the question is "what would you do" and the answer is what she will ultimately do as well. For her too many facts create a distraction and are an impediment to making a decision. It is our job as Advisors to understand this, recognize it and cater our presentation styles to the person sitting in front of us.

Along those lines, you can't have strong relationships if you pick every battle. One of my favorite sayings is "that's not a hill I'm going to die on" as it means, that's not something worth fighting for. This is something that will require good business judgement because some hills are worth dying on. For example, if a client says, "I want you to manage 1/10th of my portfolio so I can see how you do before moving over the rest" I'd say "no thank you." On the other hand, if a client says, "I don't use email so please call me or send me a letter in the mail when you want to communicate with me" I'd say, "no problem." One may be a slight imposition to my staff but it's not a fundamental conflict to my business model and it could be very important for the client.

Client Communications

Knowing what you want your business to look like and who you want to work with influences every decision you make. For example, if you work with 700 customers it makes sense to send out mass emails with generic statements like "Roth Conversions must be done by 12/31, please let us know if you are interested in doing one." This of course is not something I would ever send because my clients expect me to analyze whether they should do something. Making someone aware of something might be worth $25 per hour, analyzing whether they should do something might be worth $100 per hour. <u>Analyzing whether or not they should do something and making sure it gets done might be worth $1,000 an hour.</u>

If you want to build a $1M+ recurring revenue firm, **mass emails are not only not the way to do it but are also a detractor from the brand you may be trying to build.** The only time we send out mass emails is when we are communicating something of little importance (i.e. our office is closing at noon on Christmas Eve). Client communications are sacrosanct and so if I am recommending a client do something, they are getting a custom communication from me with follow up from me, not a mass/template email.

Mind Maps

The first time I took my FINRA Series 24 exam, I failed. I obviously hadn't studied enough but more importantly; I had no context for the material I was studying. A friend suggested that I buy a poster board and build a mind map (if you've never seen one, google image the term mind map).

Armed with a well built out mind map, I passed the 2nd time with flying colors.

Ever since that experience I've been using mind maps to help families with complex financial affairs better understand their own situation. They are an especially useful tool for Family Meetings where you may be introducing your client's adult children to levels of complexity never before imagined.

A mind map can be as simple or complex as you'd like it to be. There is specific software you can use for this or you can just use Microsoft Power Point. And these are also a great way to start meetings by taking a "big picture" approach before diving into a specific topic like gift planning or estate tax planning.

Client Segmentation

We break our clients into segments based on the annual revenue that we receive from them. Our rankings are Platinum, Gold, Silver, and Bronze. We then assign a frequency of meetings per client based on their rankings. Platinum clients get a check in 4 times per year where we offer to have them in for a meeting. Admittedly some clients want to see us this often and others don't. But from our perspective, every 90 days these clients are getting checked on. Gold clients are scheduled for 3 meetings a year, Silver twice a year and Bronze once a year. In addition to these proactive offers for a meeting, we also reach out for birthdays, special occasions (anniversary with our firm, wedding anniversary, Valentine's Day, Thanksgiving, Christmas, etc.). We also reach out whenever there is an opportunity that we want to walk a client through, this could include refinancing a mortgage, doing a Roth conversion, or updating their estate plan based on a new law or change in the tax code.

At the end of each meeting under "Next Steps" we state when we should plan to meet again. This way, much like when I leave the dentist office, the client knows when they should expect to see us again. I've found that this alleviates the stress that comes from making sure I am "checking in" frequently enough with clients. In our CRM we list the client level and the corresponding frequency with which we should be meeting. We then run a report every month showing who is "due" for a meeting and it's the Advisor's job to reach out and schedule something.

One of the things we do at Summit that I think saves a lot of time and headache is have the Advisors (myself included) manage our own calendars. I've never understood the desire to let my assistant or someone else manage my calendar, and it creates a lot of unnecessary back and forth emails with the client. When I reach out to a client for a meeting, I simply provide them my Calendly link and say something like "hopefully one of these will work but if not, feel free to suggest something else." I'd say 95% of the time one of the times I offer works. Plus, this allows me to control my own schedule and book meetings in the mornings, which is when I do my client work.

Staying Organized – Client eFiles

Every client has an electronic file folder that every member of the team has access to. Once you click on the client's name, their folder has 2 sets of subfolders. Set 1 includes:

- Correspondence
- Estate
- Financial Planning
- Forms & Applications
- Insurance
- Investments
- Taxes

Then within each of these folders, there is another set of subfolders. I won't go into all of them but here are some examples:

- Estate
  - Documents
  - Gifting

- o Internal Analysis
- Financial Planning
  - o Business Planning
  - o Meetings & Follow Up
  - o Mortgage & Debt Information
  - o Retirement Needs Analysis & Cash Flow

One of the biggest pitfalls I see with other Advisors (this includes not only Financial Advisors but CPAs and Attorneys too) is that not being organized wastes your time and the client's time and does not go unnoticed by the client. I've had numerous occasions where an Attorney emailed a mutual client asking for a document that they had already asked for and received. The client gets frustrated being asked for the same documents multiple times and it reveals how unorganized or unprofessional the Attorney may be.

The best way to combat this is to not only create these eFiles but use them religiously. Every single time we receive a document related to someone's mortgage; it gets saved in the 'Mortgage & Debt Information' subfolder. Everyone on the team knows this, and when it comes time to find a document for a client (because they are applying for a loan), anyone on the team can assist because everyone knows where everything is saved.

Several of the examples I can give for what I call "5 star service" stems from the organization and maintenance of this eFile system. I've had clients applying for a mortgage and need a K1 from 3 years ago that they couldn't find. We are able to save them all sorts of headaches by being able to easily produce it for their mortgage broker.

A quick word about these client meetings and what that process looks like:

- Our CRM system generates a report that tells me John Doe is due for a client meeting.
- I reach out to John and we schedule something for some time in the next 1-3 weeks.
- Our Director of Financial Planning (Jennifer) meets with me every week and we discuss my upcoming client meetings.
- Jennifer prepares for each meeting based on our discussion, which could be "this is a standard annual review for a bronze client who is retired" or "the client wants to come in to talk about making some changes to his estate plan". Her preparation is varied based on what I'm going to discuss with the client. Often, there is nothing she needs to prepare because in that second example, we already have an estate plan summary on file for the client and a beneficiary designation review spreadsheet. All I need to do is listen to the clients concerns and speak to what changes he could make to accomplish his new goals.
- With the client file under Financial Planning/ Meetings, a subfolder is created with the date for each meeting. In that subfolder I find all the documents that she has prepared for that meeting.
- I meet with the client and take notes.
- I send the client an email summarizing our meeting, with bullet points. Action items are highlighted and

underlined, and my Associate Geoff is copied on the email.

- Geoff then takes these action items and creates a task in our project management software which is called SmartQ. Some tasks Geoff can handle immediately without further discussion. Others are discussed at our weekly 1-1 which occurs on Monday mornings and is driven by what's listed as projects in SmartQ.
- I print the email I had sent to the client to PDF, and I scan my meeting notes. I attach these two documents together into one PDF and name it "Date/Client Name/Meeting notes and summary email". I save this file in the sub-folder that was created for the specific meeting. When Jennifer prepares for my next meeting with that client, she starts by reading my notes and email summary of the last meeting. Any item on this list that didn't get accomplished is listed on the next meeting agenda to ensure it doesn't fall off the radar (this wouldn't be a task we were supposed to accomplish but rather something the client could only do on their end -i.e., ask their benefits person for a copy of their disability policy at work).

Proactive Outreach in Between Meetings

In our CRM we track things like who has a mortgage and at what interest rate. We then create spreadsheets that allow us to see targeted opportunities, like who should be refinancing their mortgage. Because every client has an eFile which contains all their pertinent financial information, the refinance process looks something like this:

1. Email a recent copy of the client's mortgage statement to an independent mortgage broker that I've used for years and get a quote (client specific info redacted).
2. Email or call the client and ask if they are interested in refinancing, providing them with the quote and a few options (extend loan duration, keep current payment but lower rate to pay off sooner).
3. Once the client agrees, make an email introduction between them and the mortgage broker.
4. The mortgage broker then replies all with a list of items needed to get started. Because we have nearly everything on file, we send it all over so all the client has to do is send the few things we might not have.

Needless to say, the entire process is a value-add from the client's perspective. We get nothing out of it from the mortgage broker except the fact that we know they will take great care of our clients and that's payment enough.

Active listening leads to better gifts which lead to greater loyalty

In Robert Slater's book Ovitz: The Inside Story of Hollywood's Most Controversial Power Broker he tells story after story about things Michael Ovitz has done to build a loyal client base. The biggest of course being to create new income opportunities for his clients, which as an Agent is his job. But a smaller and more interesting example is how Michael consistently shocked his clients by proving them very personalized and custom gifts that were specific to their interests. So, for example rather than buy season tickets to the Lakers and assume all of his clients were basketball fans, he would take detailed notes on things that came up in conversation and then look for ways to offer a gift that was specific to that person's interests.

Years ago during our annual business planning meeting we made a list of every client we had taken on in the past 24 months and where they came from. 90%+ had come to us from larger firms. Needless to say these larger firms have larger marketing departments and more resources. So we asked ourselves, what do these clients all have in common? The answer was, they felt small at their previous firms. They were one of many. They didn't feel important.

One of the ways you can compete with "the big boys" is through active listening. I had a client once tell me that the best vacation he ever took was to a town in Scotland named Oban because that was his favorite thing to drink, and he loved Scotland. 10 months later I saw on my calendar that his 75th birthday was approaching so I bought him a bottle of Oban and delivered it to him. He was shocked that I had remembered.

Another time I had a client tell me that for his 60th birthday (which was almost a year away) he and his wife were going to Europe for the 1st time ever. Knowing that their trip was still on, 30 days before their trip I sent them a care package of items one might want when visiting Europe – travel voltage converters, a money belt, some Rick Steve's books, etc.

The clients called me as soon as the package arrived, shocked that I had remembered.

The key to all of this is to listen actively when clients tell you something important. Take notes in CRM and set reminders in your calendar for events that may seem far away in the distant future. **Everyone wants to be heard.**

Cash Flow Planning

Second only to understanding a client's goals, comes understanding a client's cash flows. I know some firms use a budget worksheet for this, others (like ours) use a combination of sources such as their tax returns, paystubs, and year over year changes in cash levels and debt levels. Meaning we try to figure out our client's cash flows for them without asking them to complete a budget worksheet. The one exception is when a client is entering retirement. I've found that most people think they will spend much less in retirement, presumably because they read that somewhere. We put that to the test by having them use the MoneyGuidePro® budget worksheet which compares, by category, current expenses to what you think they will be in retirement.

We do cash flow planning in two different ways – with financial planning software and in Microsoft Excel. The financial planning software does a great job of projecting what will happen over 20-year or even 30-year periods of time. But for most clients, that isn't specific enough for them to get their arms around.

As a result, we have developed 3 different cash flow models:

- For HENRYs – we build a 5-year cash flow model

- For near retirees & retirees – we build a 10-year cash flow model
- For Wealth Management clients – we build both a 10-year and a 1-year (month by month) cash flow model

The reasons for this are as follows:

- For HENRYs – A lot can change over the next 5 years. Kids can migrate from paid pre-school to free elementary school, student loans can get paid off freeing up cash flow for reinvestment, etc.
- For near retirees & retirees – Everyone, even high net worth clients, worry about the transition that occurs when one goes from having a paycheck come in every month, to living off their investments. The 10-year cash flow model helps them see exactly where the money will be coming from to replace their lost paycheck.
- For Wealth Management clients – high net worth clients also enjoy seeing the year-by-year breakdown of what comes in and what goes out, but because they tend to have so many moving parts, we've found that they also like to see what will happen on a monthly basis. These folks usually have multiple homes, so we are dealing with multiple property tax bills, large quarterly estimated tax payments, tuition bills for grandkids, etc.

Bar none, the one visual aid that clients ask me to print above all others is their cash flow model. I can show them with certainty that their financial planning projections show a 99% success rate, and rarely do they ask for that report – but nearly every time they ask me for a copy of their cash flow report. I've even had one couple tell me that they taped theirs to the fridge.

Investments

"If you spend more than 13 minutes a year on market forecasts, you've wasted 10 minutes" - Peter Lynch

You can be an investment advisor and not a financial advisor. However, you cannot be a financial advisor and not also an investment advisor. Investments are the engine that makes the whole thing work.

My thinking around investing other people's money as part of an overall financial plan is as follows:

- Always remember, you are managing a client's hard-earned wealth. You should not speculate with someone else's money, and you should have a good understanding of what you are doing and why. That may seem obvious but at a lot of firms Advisors are pressured to "bring in assets" and then let someone else manage them. We can get into that a bit more later but for now, it's not good enough to let someone else manage investments if you don't understand what they are doing. Again, you don't have to be a CFA® Charter Holder but you have to ask good questions and understand the risks involved. At the end of the day the client is looking to you to be the expert and pointing the finger at someone else isn't going to be good enough.

- You need to have a philosophy around how money should be managed, and you need to communicate this philosophy with your clients and stick to it when managing their portfolios. An example of a philosophy could be "I believe in using low-cost index funds and rebalancing once a year." Another could be "I believe in picking money managers who have shown the ability to outperform on a risk adjusted basis over time." I am not here to dispute whatever philosophy you subscribe to. But I will tell you this – absent an investment philosophy, you will go wherever the wind takes you. You will be impressed by whatever the wholesaler in front of you has to say, or the portfolio manager you just heard on the podcast you were listening to.

- You need to have a robust process for managing someone's hard-earned wealth. (Our 6-step process is listed just below).

- You must be firm with new clients when setting expectations around time frames and performance. In one of Harold Evensky's books he said he tells new clients, "If you won't let me manage your money for 5 years, don't let me manage it for a day." I've stolen this line from Harold and used it for years. For some clients (younger ones) I will tell them, "don't ask me to manage any money that you want back for the next 10 years." I also tell new clients that in the 1st year of review meetings, we will not even talk about performance, good or bad. It's not that we are hiding it, it's simply that the time period is too small to be relevant.

Listen Carefully

When you are young and clients and assets are scarce, you will sometimes hear what you want to hear from a prospective client. As you get older, wiser, and burned a time or two, this changes. The best example I can give is that when a prospective client reaches out, I will talk to them about their current Advisory relationship (if they have one) and what they don't like about their Advisor. If the answer is the fact that their current Advisor either doesn't do planning or doesn't return their calls/emails in a timely manner, then I will keep the conversation going. However, if I hear anything performance related, my antennae goes up. Now granted there are some bad Advisors out there just like there are bad apples in any bunch, and sometimes their performance concerns are justified. But not always and the last thing I will ever do is a sell a prospective client on the idea that my performance is better than the other guy's performance and that's why they should fire their Advisor and hire me. Even if I believe that to be true, I will never sell someone on that premise. As Nick Murray likes to say, we manage money in service to a plan. If a prospective client wants someone to design, implement and monitor their plan, including managing their portfolio, then we are interested. Anything less than that and you are just "renting the client" until some period of underperformance comes.

Our Six Step Process to Managing a Client's Portfolio

Every single investment client should go through the following process:

1. **Complete a risk profile questionnaire** (one per spouse). Notice this is not called a risk tolerance questionnaire and if you go to my website and download the one we use, you will see it doesn't look like any risk tolerance questionnaire you've ever seen. I don't like or use risk tolerance questionnaires because I've found they are subject to recency bias. When markets are hot, everyone is an aggressive investor. When markets are tanking, everyone thinks a 4%-5% annual return sounds just fine.

2. **Use planning software to determine the client's required rate of return**. This is the return they need to earn on their capital to meet their goals. Be sure to run this with varying levels of inflation as using a 2% or 3% inflation estimate can really skew the results.

3. **Educate them on how various asset classes have performed over different time periods.** If I told a client that between 2007 and 2021 a certain asset class averaged 10.58% per year and that a $1,000,000 portfolio with no withdrawals would have grown to $4,521,351, most people would say "sign me up for that". But what if I then told them that to get those kinds of returns, they had to start by digesting a 57% decline and seeing their $1,000,000 portfolio dwindle down to $430,000 in the 1st 18 months, and then from there they had to stick to

their guns and not panic sell at the bottom. If people are being honest with themselves, they will admit that after the 1st 20% decline they'd be so nervous that they'd be losing sleep at night and would probably not stick to the original plan.

    a. By this same token, when educating clients about the importance of balance and diversification in a portfolio, you must also educate them about the times when the US stock market is up 28% for the year and their boring globally diversified portfolio is "only up" 10% or 12% and that this too could lead to them wanting to abandon the plan.

4. **Write up an Investment Policy Statement** that is specific to the client and their unique situation. We call ours an Investment Strategy Statement and a template is available for download from the website. These are reviewed with the client and signed by the client and the Advisor.

5. **Show the client on an account-by-account level, what you will be investing in**, and if existing positions that came over are being sold, what the cost and tax ramifications are.

6. **Have the client sign a document at the account level detailing the risk profile for that particular account,** any cash needs or one-off circumstances that FA needs to keep in mind when managing the portfolio (i.e. no gun stocks).

What to do when the market corrects

It is March of 2020 and equity markets are declining at daily levels not seen since the crash of 1987. Client emails and calls are flooding in. The #1 question at hand is "what are you doing to protect my portfolio?"

I said earlier in the fee section of the book that the value you create for clients can be lumpy, coming in fits and spurts over the years. This is one of the times where you can create massive value by convincing clients that we should do all the following:

1. Tax loss harvest – If you are a CFP® Professional you know what this means so I won't bore you with an explanation
2. Roth conversions – same comment
3. Rebalance – what an opportunity to sell some bonds and buy some stocks
4. Invest cash that's been sitting on the sidelines

To get clients to move from panic to action you must first and foremost remind clients that volatility is the price one pays to get equity returns. Next you must remind them that they are going to be "ok" and that this is why we build portfolios the way that we do. (*Now is not the time to talk about YTD performance or even performance over the past 3 or 5 years because quite frankly, a 4-week market correction can wipe out all of the gains a client has achieved over the past few years. But this is temporary and so is our opportunity to act.*)

If you remain calm so will your clients and they will thank you later for calmy steering the ship into safe waters.

One comment here on tax-loss harvesting, I remember reading in another Advisor's book about all the value he felt his firm had added by doing tax-loss harvesting during the depths of the 2008 crash and thinking to myself "do clients really care about that stuff when their portfolios are dropping like a rock?"

The answer is, no they don't care about it while its happening, but fast forward a few years to when the gains have reemerged in their portfolios and you get to be the one to tell them that you can rebalance their portfolio and trim some equities without any capital gains taxes because you kept a level head and tax-loss harvested many moons ago when the rest of the world was on fire.

Different Investment Vehicles

- ETFs vs. Mutual Funds vs. SMAs (separately managed accounts) – I can honestly say I've tried all three at various points in my career. The argument behind ETFs is that they are cheap, simple to understand, and tax efficient. They are also easy to manage if you are doing things like tax-loss harvesting. If you are using ETFs, your value-add, as it relates to investments, is seemingly your asset allocation. However, as we discussed above, your real value add is almost always related to action and not to information. Meaning anyone can google an asset allocation and copy whatever they find. Few can stick with it when the chips are down. Few will rebalance into an out of favor asset class after years of underperformance. Few will trim their winners after years of outperformance.

This is $1,000 an hour work and this is something you must be able to do as an FA.

The argument behind using active mutual funds is as follows:

- You can add value by identifying active managers that can outperform their benchmarks.
- You can build a world-class portfolio and team of portfolio managers by combining different mutual funds.
- You can show a long-term track record of historic performance (often not the case with newer ETFs) and in theory this will motivate clients to act in the first place AND to stick with their portfolios when the chips are down.

My co-worker who is an extremely successful FA uses active mutual funds and has for years, so I can't say I object to any of the aforementioned bullet points. For me, I like blending low cost-tax efficient ETFs with the occasional Alternative Investment. Mutual funds are always more expensive and less tax efficient than ETFs. Plus, the only way a mutual fund can beat its benchmark is by having a high Active Share which means investments that deviate from the benchmark. This deviation or Active Share can lead to great outperformance but also leads to great underperformance. This leaves you as the Advisor in a position where you must judge whether the style of the MF manager is simply out of favor or whether changes at the firm or in the manager's person life have impacted his/her mojo. I've heard of institutional money managers tracking things like a portfolio manager's golf handicap as a proxy for how much they are actually working and use that as evidence against them when the fund is underperforming. Finally, it's harder to tax loss harvest with active mutual funds for reasons that are hopefully obvious to a CFP® Professional.

SMAs are basically tax efficient mutual funds with higher minimums. The appeal of SMAs is the argument that you can get the client access to world class money managers that don't want to manage grandma's $2,500 Roth IRA. However, the logistics and the fees involved are the biggest detractor in my opinion. For example, we have placed money with a firm that mirrors various equity indices but with a tax overlay that includes daily tax-loss harvesting. We also place money with a firm that specializes in CA municipal bonds. Let's assume a client starts with 60% of their money in the equity fund and 40% in the CA Muni fund. A year later the equity fund now has 72% of the portfolio and the CA Muni fund has 28%. To rebalance I need to get client paperwork to move money from one firm to the other. Clearly this is more of a logistical problem than I would have if I were managing a portfolio with ETFs all inside of one account.

In-sourcing vs. Outsourcing trading & portfolio management – Here is another area where I've tried it both ways and different variants within each way. The argument for outsourcing portfolio management is that your job is to bring in new clients and manage relationships, not watch every tick of the stock market. The argument for in-sourcing portfolio management is that you should be the one making the investment decisions as you know the client and the client may want, need, or expect some degree of customization which is very hard to do when you outsource this function. The other argument against outsourcing is that you are stacking an investment management firm's fee on top of your fee and suddenly, the client may be paying 2% or more for a portfolio of index funds/ETFs.

Given that I've tried both, I believe that the answer is to in-source but with enough economies of scale that you can hire a full-time PM (portfolio manager) and a trader.

Let's look at some math as an example:

> You manage $100M of assets with a weighted average fee of 0.70% (based on the idea that some clients will have more than $1M and that above $1M your fee drops below 1%.
>
> That means you are generating $700K per year in AUM revenue. Let's say you were to outsource portfolio management to a TAMP (Turnkey Asset Management Provider) and that this firm's all-in cost is around 0.6% per year, on top of your asset management fee.
>
> Your clients are now paying an additional $600,000 per year in fees.
>
> Suppose instead you hired a Portfolio Manager and a Trader and paid them $250K and $100K respectively. Now you are getting the same access but for less than

2/3 of the price. And the cost savings is being borne by your clients.

This is the route we've gone, and we did by: A. raising some client fees along the way (and by using real numbers to do so) and B. bringing in more AUM so that our revenue was increasing without a commensurate increase in the costs of portfolio management and trading.

The argument for outsourcing is that someone else is having to make the big decisions around asset allocation and you have one or two less people to employ & manage. You also have someone else to blame when things don't go as planned. For me, none of these benefits are worth losing the customization that comes with in-sourcing. First, I don't think you can really blame a 3rd party money manager for poor results if you were the one that hired them in the first place. Second, conversations around keeping a legacy position for tax purposes or excluding a specific industry because the client already has a large concentration in that sector are easier to have and manage when my PM and my trader sit down the hall from me. I'm also more informed on what they are thinking and what they are seeing because I am talking to them every day.

Tax Loss Harvesting (TLH) – Lesson Learned

In life, it's always better to learn the painful lessons from someone else vs. experiencing them firsthand. It's one of the reasons we as parents are always trying to teach our kid's what not to do.

One of my friends in the industry taught me a painful lesson that he learned the hard way around tax-loss harvesting that has transformed the way we handle TLH transactions in our office.

In late December one year after a brutal quarter, his firm decided to tax loss harvest at year-end to at least provide some tax relief to offset how bad the month-end statements would look. The issue came up when they realized that they had one very large mutual fund that they weren't quite sure how to handle. You see, tax-loss harvesting is easy when you are swapping one large cap index fund for another, but what about more esoteric investments? Their portfolio models all held a unique mutual fund with no obvious substitute investment.

Not knowing what to do, they decided to book the loss and then sit on cash for the intervening 31 days, knowing that after that period they would buy back into the fund. Lo and behold, the fund was up 11% in the month that they sat out. That single month performance was better than the fund's performance for the entire previous year, and their clients missed it.

The point here should be obvious but just in case it isn't – **for every single investment in your portfolio, make sure you identify a substitute fund well in advance.** Even if the correlation is not 0.99, participating in some upside over the wash-sale window time period is better than sitting on the sidelines.

Tax Planning

If you are reading this you are likely a CFP® Professional so I won't explain to you what tax planning is or why it's important, but rather how it gets done at a firm like ours. First, we own and operate two separate legal entities- Summit Wealth & Retirement Partners is an S Corp that is a dually registered RIA and has a broker-dealer affiliation. Summit Tax Planning is an S Corp that offers tax preparation, tax consulting and bookkeeping.

<u>Fall Tax Prep -</u> For mock tax returns and projections we use a software called **Holistiplan**. Holistiplan came on my radar after hearing their founder interviewed on the Michael Kitces podcast. I was so impressed that I immediately signed up for a trial and we've never looked back. With Holistiplan you can scan and upload a client's existing tax returns and then use that as a baseline from which to create alternate scenarios. Prior to having this software, we used Drake, Lacerte and BNA Income Tax Planner. All good solutions but all of which required us to manually build the baseline tax return first before we could create alternative versions. For some client's that was easy but for most, that was the hardest part of the entire exercise.

Everything that we do at Summit is calendared. So come September 1st we look at a list of who received a mock tax return in the previous year and then which new clients have been added to our roster since. Between these two we come up with a list of who should have a mock tax return for the current year. Bronze clients don't get mock tax returns and some Platinum clients already get these from their CPA, so we don't create them ourselves for fear of stepping on toes.

This target list is then separated into those that are still working from those that are not.

For those that are still working, an email goes out asking for YTD paystubs and anything else we should know about before we build their tax projections (I will use mock tax returns and tax projections inter-changeably as they mean the same thing). For retired or independently wealthy clients, we may need to get a YTD realized gain loss report from an outside money manager (many of our clients are invested in hedge funds or limited partnerships not at Schwab).

Once we have what we need we create the mock tax return for the current year and look for opportunities. Because we have a 10-year cash flow projection for every client, we also compare the current year's projections to the 10-year. This will then lead to conversations like:

- Roth conversions
- Tax gain harvesting (tax loss harvesting is done automatically on our end)
- Gifting appreciated stock to charity
- Setting up a donor advised fund
- Noticing that a client is not on track to max out their 401K and having them reduce their paycheck for the balance of the year to ensure this gets done

We host either an in-person meeting or a zoom meeting where we walk the client through their mock tax return and discuss specific recommendations. Sometimes there is nothing they can do differently and that's ok too. Sometimes the process simply leads to showing them they are expected to owe a lot come April and then we discuss where that $ will come from and what led to an under withholding. If for example it's the client's first year in retirement, they may have chosen not to withhold taxes from Social Security. At that point we can discuss whether they want to pay estimated taxes throughout their retirement or if they'd prefer, we over withhold from their IRA distributions to offset the Social Security income. The simple fact that we are on top of these things helps the clients achieve the worry-free retirement that we promised them when they hired us.

<u>Spring Tax Prep -</u> In January we send out an email that reminds clients that Schwab 1099s usually come out twice so that they shouldn't assume the first one they receive is their final. We also then remind them that if our firm is preparing their tax returns, we will review them before the client sees them, but that if our firm is **not** preparing their tax returns, they need to ask their CPA to send us a draft before they finalize them. We send our client's 1099s directly to their CPAs (whether we do their taxes or not) and we have a document on file, signed by each client, authorizing us to do so. When we send these to the CPA's we also remind them that we want a copy of the draft tax return before its

completed. Between the CPA and the client, I'd say 95% of the time we get to see a copy before its finalized.

When we review the client's tax return, we compare it to the mock return we prepared in the fall as well as our cash flow projections. You would be amazed at how often we find mistakes on the draft. For example, we might have done an IRA rollover and for whatever reason it was coded on the tax return as a distribution. I've seen a client with 6 figures of municipal bond income and the CPA coded the entire thing as taxable income. Other times it will be little things like we know the client had some major health issues or did major renovations to their rental home the previous year but then when we look at the Schedule A or the Schedule E those expenses aren't listed. Sometimes the client forgot to give them to the CPA and sometimes the CPA just missed getting them on the return. We also give the CPA the benefit of the doubt and remind the clients that the CPA is trying to do several hundred returns in a limited time period, and therefore we need to review their return before its finalized.

The high value stuff - For most of our HENRYs and Near Retirees/Retirees, the stuff we've already mentioned covers most of our work around tax planning. But for our Wealth Management clients there is a whole other world that exists for high end tax planning. Most of these ideas are outside the scope of this book but do yourself a favor and get smart about CRTs, upstream gifting, and downstream gifting. I will give you a simple example – in 2019 we had a client who was sitting on a large unrealized gain in a single stock. He said he wanted to sell the stock and use the proceeds to help his daughter buy a car and his son pay off his student loans.

We walked him through 2 options for accomplishing this task:

- Option 1 – sell the stock, pay the taxes, gift the proceeds.
- Option 2 – we set up Schwab accounts for each of his kids. We gift the stock to his kids, and they sell half the shares in the present year and the rest in the coming year and then use the money for those same purposes.
- We ran mock tax returns for him showing the tax impact of selling the stock as well as mock tax returns showing the tax impact of his kids selling the stock over 2 years. Both of his kids were grown adults who were supporting themselves and paying their own way. However, our tax code and the tax rate on capital gains varies from 0% to 23.8% depending upon your income. Not to mention California taxes capital gains as ordinary income.
- After seeing that option 2 would save about $25,000 in taxes, the client went for option 2.
- This meant we:
  - Set up 2 new Schwab accounts
  - Journaled the shares
  - Sold ½ the stock in each account in the current year
  - Sold the balance in the next year

- Wired the $ needed for the son to pay off his student loans and for the daughter to buy a car
- Held conference calls with each child asking them what they wanted to do with the remaining funds. The daughter asked us to manage them for her, the son wanted to withdraw the funds and use them for other purposes (which his parents were ok with)
- We sent copies of everything to the client's CPA who filed a gift tax return for them

This is a simple example of the kind of work we are doing every single day. This constitutes real tax planning whereas many of your competitors say they do tax planning but all they are really doing is using municipal bonds instead of corporate bonds in after-tax accounts. Clients know the difference between what we do, and it leads to stickier relationships and greater assets under management.

That time I bought a Tax Business

In 2014 I decided that I was done courting CPAs and was going to simply buy an existing tax practice and integrate it with my wealth management business. I went to a website called APS.net (accounting practice sales) and started searching for one in my area. I found one about 10 miles away selling for just over 1.25 times revenue. I filled out the acquisition questionnaire and quickly received a call back from the broker. He told me the seller (let's call him 'Richard') had bought the business just 6 months earlier from the original company founder, who ran it successfully for over 30 years. Of course, all sorts of red flags went up as to why the seller was ready to part ways just 6 months after his purchase.

I went and met with Richard and toured his offices. He said he had been a corporate accountant his entire career and completed 30+ tax returns "on the side" for friends and family. After a series of job changes and layoffs, he finally decided to just turn his avocation into his vocation. Just a few months in he realized he had made a mistake – he was not cut out to be an entrepreneur. Turns out he had borrowed the money to buy the business and was now losing sleep over the debt.

Interestingly enough, he said his ideal scenario would be to sell the business and then stay on as an employee, or what we now call a "Sell and stay".

Fittingly enough, I wanted to own a tax practice but had (and still have) zero interest in preparing tax returns.

Given this I was ready to start the due diligence process, which is beyond the scope of this section, but I do think it's worth mentioning one thing – my assumptions.

I assumed that buying a tax practice would confer 3 benefits to my clients, my business, and myself personally:

1. I wanted to be able to refer my clients to an in-house tax preparer and control the price they paid to have their taxes completed. I had seen clients pay thousands of dollars for simple returns and knew that was an area of opportunity and a way to save them money.
2. I wanted to stop trying to educate multiple CPAs around town as to why they should refer clients to me

and instead focus on educating one CPA why he should be referring clients to me. My thinking was the tax practice completes 300 returns a year. Assume 10% of those folks will need my service (a conservative assumption) and with the CPA's blessing, 50% of them would hire me. Back then my average revenue per client was around $8K per year so that's 15 clients X $8K = $120K of new revenue plus a new pipeline of future referrals from the in-house CPA.

3. I wanted a stream of income that wouldn't be tied to the stock market. Every investor is seeking uncorrelated investments and as a financial advisor, our livelihood and our investment portfolios are all tied to the stock market. I figured it would make sense to diversify and buy an asset where the income stream had nothing to do with the stock market. Seeing that the tax practice was profitable, this seemed to make sense.

So, I did what any young naïve person would do, I took a home equity loan to buy a tax practice. My oldest son was 5, my middle son was 3, and my wife was pregnant. It had been two years since I had left my previous job and taken a 60% pay cut to join my current firm and my buyout negotiations with the founder of the wealth management business were not exactly going according to plan. Needless to say, my wife was a bit nervous.

Things with 'Richard' didn't exactly go according to plan and my assumptions for how many tax clients would hire us was off by 90%, but 8 years later I can say buying the tax practice was one of the better decisions we ever made. It added a ton of value for our existing clients and continues to help us win new business from prospective clients who love the "one-stop-shop" concept. And because the business has remained profitable, I was able to pay back that home equity line and now have that non correlated income stream that I had hoped for.

Estate Planning

You cannot be a real financial planner if you don't address estate planning with your clients.

For younger clients, that can be as simple as making sure they have current documents in place where they've named guardians for young children, trustees for the money they would be leaving behind to those young children and making sure everything is titled correctly so that their plan works properly.

For retirees and wealth management clients, your role as it comes to estate planning includes everything from making sure the documents are current (and still reflect the client's wishes) to making sure the beneficiaries are correct to having those sometimes-difficult conversations around their heir's ability to inherit money. By this point they know if their kids are frugal or spendthrifts, if they have health or mental issues, if they have soon to be ex-spouses, etc. These are difficult conversations to have but if you want to work in wealth management, they are part of the job.

For clients with an existing estate plan, we read all their documents and diagram a summary of what will happen should anything happen to them and who will play critical roles all on one piece of paper. Clients love this and tell me it's the first time they've ever really understand the meaning of "all those documents they signed" that have been sitting in a binder ever since. Once we review this, either the client suggests changes (based on what they know about family members or something else that is no longer current) or we suggest changes based on changes in net worth or estate tax law since their documents were created.

For clients without an existing estate plan, we use an Estate Planning Intake Form (available on our website) to get an understanding of their estate planning wishes. We tell them verbally, and this document clearly states, <u>that we are not estate planning attorneys</u>. Our job is not to replace their estate planning attorney or to draft documents. We are simply trying to save them time and money by quarterbacking the estate planning process.

Once their Estate Planning Intake Form is completed (with ample coaching from us, questions around using just a survivor's trust at first death to incorporating a bypass or marital trust are all part of the discussion), we then send the Intake Form and the Client's Net Worth Statement to the attorney. In that email we tell the attorney what documents are needed and what provisions we've discussed and agreed to with the client.

Having done this for many years there is no doubt that the estate planning attorneys appreciate the legwork that we've done because it makes their lives easier and the clients we send over actually complete their estate plans. I can also say that clients thank us profusely for guiding them through this process because, often it was something they've been meaning to do for years but either never got around to it or were too intimated by the whole thing to know where to start.

Wrapping Up

For the sake of brevity, I've touched on just a few areas of financial planning so that you could see how the process takes place in real life. I've purposely not covered every single area but can assure you that we have a similar process in place for all of the following areas for clients:

- Insurance planning 1 – life, disability, long-term care
- Insurance planning 2 – property & casualty
- College planning
- Charitable planning
- Asset protection planning

While we've only scratched the surface here, we want to make it clear that Wealth management = Investment Management + Wealth Protection + Wealth Transfer + Tax Planning + Charitable Planning, all fully integrated and customized for the client's benefit.

SECTION III

BUILDING AND MAINTAINING A PROFESSIONAL STAFF OF 'A' PLAYERS

My Initial Staff at Summit

When reading about all the things we do for our clients, I realize it may sound overwhelming. And it would be if I didn't have a team of "A" players helping me every step along the way.

When I took over the firm our entire staff consisted entirely of "B" and "C" players. Everything was difficult. We either didn't have a process or we had one and didn't have the discipline to follow it. Over an 18-month period I replaced every single staff member and every single piece of software we used. *I eventually changed broker-dealers as well and moved the office, but we can save that for another discussion.* The point being, when I changed the composition of the team to all "A" players – **everything changed.**

Author and Podcast Host Tim Ferris likes to say "what's the one problem you could tackle (in your business, in life) that would make every other problem that much easier to solve. Well, I can say for certain, in business the answer is <u>hiring and maintaining a staff of all "A" players.</u>

When it comes to hiring and maintaining a team, I take my advice from Dr. Laura who says, "Choose wisely, treat kindly". She was talking about spouses, but the same advice applies for your staff.

Choosing wisely is harder than you think so I will give you just a few suggestions on things that have worked for me:

- Write the job description first and then hire to it. Think about the personality type it takes to be good at certain jobs. A bookkeeper for example should be very good with attention to detail. Someone in charge of new business development should be creative and outgoing.
- Use a multi-step screening process that includes more than just interviews

  o Step 1 would be to collect resumes and require a cover memo. Simply requiring a cover memo will eliminate a lot of candidates that just blindly apply for jobs without really understanding the company or the role.
  o Step 2 would be a zoom interview or phone call. This is a preliminary interview, and I am just screening to see if they show up, show up on time, and show up prepared.

o Step 3 would be to then give them one or two personality tests. We like the DISC profile and the Kolbe. Each of these will cost you about $50 but remember two things:

- You are only giving these tests to people that have already made it through your first two screens
- If you are going to "choose wisely" you need to invest some time and money on the front end because training the wrong person and then having to terminate them is much worse than "wasting money" on personality tests.

o Step 4 would be an in-person interview where they are having to respond to specific situations (i.e. how would you handle the following email from a client)

- Remember the adage, "hire slow, fire fast". Almost all bad hiring decisions stem from having not spent enough time with the candidate on the front-end.

o Step 5 is where they meet the rest of the team. While I am not looking for consensus necessarily, I am looking for cultural fit plus I don't want my team to think they were not a part of the decision-making process.

Beginning with the End in Mind

When it comes to job descriptions, it helps to think about **what the team will ultimately look like**. This is where the Stephen Covey phrase "begin with the end in mind" comes into play.

Think about the end product you want to deliver to your clients and work backwards. For example, if you want to own & operate a firm that helps high net worth clients engage in annual tax planning, you will need someone on the team who has expertise in this area. You might also need a support person who can request tax related documents from clients and then enter information into tax planning software.

To that end, it's probably a good time to start thinking about what type of Advisory Firm you want to own.

Different Types of Advisory Firms

From the outside looking in, it's probably very hard to tell the difference between all the myriad Financial Services firms. Here is my attempt to categorize them.

- **Transaction or Product Based** – This would be North-western Mutual, Mass Mutual, or even the Wirehouse firms that still earn a commission when they sell a product (loaded mutual fund, UIT, etc.).
- **Project Based or Hourly** – these are your NAPFA (national association of personal financial advisors) who charge a flat hourly fee for advice. These folks are still a small segment of the industry, but I mention

them because these folks are an exact 180 of the transaction or product based advisors.

- **Relationship Based firms** - In the middle of this spectrum (and where I firmly recommend you place yourself) is Relationship Based firms. This would be any firm where an FA has an ongoing relationship with a client and receives ongoing compensation for their advice & expertise. Remember to contrast that vs. being paid each time you meet/talk to someone (either because you charge an hourly fee or because the purpose of your calls is to sell product).

  o **If your goal is to build a $1M recurring revenue firm, relationship based is the only way to go, in my opinion.** Transaction-based firms are always on the treadmill and every conversation they have with clients is centered around what product can be sold next. It doesn't take clients long to pick up on this and trust diminishes quickly. Without trust, there is no relationship.

Within the relationship-based firms one can choose to operate as an RIA only or as a Hybrid firm (RIA coupled with a broker-dealer relationship) or as a Multi-Family Offices. An RIA cannot receive any commissions, so they cannot sell insurance and can only sell limited kinds of annuities. A hybrid means you are dually registered with the state or SEC for your RIA and you have your FINRA licenses (Series 7 for example) with a broker-dealer. That broker-dealer gives you access to sell commission-based products. A multi-family

Office is designed to work with a small number of ultra-high net worth families and usually provides services that go beyond what traditional RIAs or Hybrid firms provide.

Our business is a hybrid within a hybrid as we are dually registered (RIA and broker-dealer) and we provide many of the services that a multi-family office would provide (family literacy coaching for client's kids, tax return preparation, business planning, family meetings, etc.).

This book is geared for Advisors that want a relationship-based practice. I don't like the product/transaction-based business model because its often more about the Advisor getting paid than what's best for the client. I don't like the project-based practice because most clients will not act on the advice they receive from an hourly planning session. I understand why this form of business model appeals to some, but in my experience telling a client what they <u>should</u> do is worth $200 an hour. **<u>Making sure it actually gets done is worth $1,000 an hour</u>**. My time is limited so I'd rather work with fewer clients and be responsible for making sure that what we recommend gets done.

Personality Profiles & The Career Path

If you hire ambitious people, they are going to seek opportunities for career advancement. If you or your firm cannot provide such opportunities, then you will be training these people only for some other firm to benefit from your work.

We are clear with our employees about what the career path looks like in the industry and at our firm. We also make it clear as to what is necessary to advance.

When you look at a person's DISC profile and their Kolbe you will get a better sense of how ambitious they are and can prepare accordingly.

If you go to our website you can download our career path and edit it as you see fit for your firm.

In addition, I feel strongly that promoting from within is infinitely better and more likely to succeed than hiring from the outside. I also feel strongly that when hiring, attitude and habits are far more important than industry experience. **We can teach the right person everything that they need to know about the particular job but you cannot teach someone to have the right attitude or the right habits**. When interviewing, focus on these two traits and you will be pleasantly surprised by the outcome.

To that end, a bit about mentoring:

The One Page Guide to Mentoring

In 2006 I was attending a LAMP Conference in Toronto (LAMP stands for leaders and managers program and is specifically for the financial services industry). One of the statistics that jumped out at me was that 85% of new advisors fail within the first 3 years. When I got back to California, I told our leadership team that our new goal was to flip this number on its head and see that 85% of our new Advisors succeed and make it past the 3-year mark. The thinking there being that if you make it past that milestone, you've made it in this profession (granted the fun is just beginning at that point but at least you are no longer worried about starving out of the business).

After many brainstorming sessions and studying what did and didn't work, we decided that there were 2 things we could do to greatly improve the odds of success for a new Advisor:

1. Hire them onto a team from day 1.
2. Assign them a mentor and require that the mentor and mentee draft and sign a 2-page **document of expectations.** On page 1 the mentor would spell out what he/she would provide to the mentee. On page 2 the mentor would spell out what he/she would expect from the mentee.

In this document both parties would agree exactly when they would meet each week to review this document (Fridays at 10am for example).

In this document parties would spell out what the plan was if either side wasn't living up to their end of the bargain.

Finally, in this document both parties would identify who would mediate if things were not going according to plan.

With respect to the details, let me give you some examples:

From the Mentor:

- I will allow you to sit in all internal financial strategy meetings where I discuss ideas and opportunities for new clients
- I will allow you to shadow me on Wednesdays and I will conduct 3+ client meetings on those days

- I will give you the names and phone numbers of 30 "C" clients for you to call
- I will dedicate Monday afternoons from 2-3 to discuss opportunities with you, role play scenarios, discuss technical items you've read.

To the Mentee:

- I expect you to be in the office Monday through Friday (unless out on appointments with me) from 8am to 5pm
- I expect you to complete 1 CFP course every 3 months until sitting for the final exam
- I expect you to spend 5 hours per week, outside the office, studying (either CFP materials or other reading)
- I expect you to attend one industry webinar per week and take notes
- I will evaluate you and expect you to evaluate yourself based on a K.A.S.H. system:

  * Knowledge
  * Attitude
  * Skills
  * Habits

The K.A.S.H. framework helps both parties by establishing what is expected over various time frames. For example the Knowledge section might say "Complete one CFP® course every 90 days".

I can tell you, within 12 months of implementing these 2 ideas we hit our goal. And 10 years later my former firm is still adhering to this same policy and still has an 85% success rate with new Advisors.

Compensation for Team Members

Before joining my current firm, I was a player/coach for a large independent broker-dealer. In that role I served 80 Advisors as their Managing Director while also managing a large staff. In talking one day with the home office about compensation for our staff members, I learned that large Fortune 500 companies have a philosophy when it comes to compensation. The philosophy at the firm I worked for was to figure out the range of pay for a given job and pay the median wage for the role. When it was my turn to speak I let the person from Human Resources who shared this information with me know that this was the dumbest thing I had ever heard. Who wants to work at a company that has a goal of paying their employees average wages?

With that in mind, I knew that when I was in charge of my own firm, my philosophy on compensation would be just the opposite. We use compensation studies from firms like Charles Schwab and Investment News to figure out what each role on the team typically earns in the marketplace. Then we set our goal to pay the higher end of that range. We do so by combining both fixed and variable compensation into our comp package and I talk a bit more about this later in the book in the section titled 65/15/20.

To add just a few more comments on my Compensation Philosophy

- I'd rather have 6 A+ players than 12 B players even if it means I'm paying my folks 2 X the average pay.

- Partners earn a below average salary but share in corporate profits + participation in a corporate profit sharing plan (PSP) + participation in a corporate pension plan (Cash Balance) + a 401K contribution + Health Ins.
- Advisors receive a % of the revenue they produce and/or are assigned + a 401K contribution + Health Ins.
- Advisors compensation is also:
    - Based on a grid
    - They pay no expenses out of pocket
    - Participate in PSP + CB plan but it is self-funded
    - Team Members earn an above average salary + PSP + CB Plan + 401K + Health Ins. + 30 PTO days a year *(which of course no one ever actually takes)*
- Investment News and major custodians like Charles Schwab put out annual compensation studies. You should be reading these and using them to help you determine base salaries and target compensation for your team members.

The Structure of our Team

As of the time of this writing, our firm structure is as follows:
- 2 Managing Partners
- 2 Financial Advisors
- 1 COO/CCO
- 1 Director of Financial Planning

- 1 Director of Tax Planning
- 2 Full-Time Service Associates
- 1 Finance Manager/Administrative Support Person

I believe that this represents a true Ensemble firm, as outlined by Philip Palaveev in several of his books and magazine articles.

What makes this structure work is the following:

- The Director of Financial Planning and the Director of Tax Planning are both shared resources, available equally to the entire firm and all clients of the firm. This creates a lot of synergies and avoids duplication of efforts and analysis around certain topics (i.e. once a template is built for how to think about something like Roth conversions or when to take social security, this can easily be scaled across the firm).
- The Full-Time Service Associates are divided into 2 different teams, so they each get used to working with specific Advisors and this limits the number of Advisors who are assigning work to them.
- The Administrative Support Person handles a set of tasks for everyone, which again avoids inefficiency and duplication of efforts.
- The COO manages all of these individuals and is also the CCO, which means that compliance is a consideration in every aspect of our operations.

Wrapping Up

Your firm philosophy around hiring, mentoring and compensation will feed directly into your firm culture.

Alabama's famous football coach Nick Saban likes to say "Mediocre people don't like high achievers and high achievers don't like mediocre people." I cannot emphasize this quote enough when it comes to building and maintaining your team. You cannot allow even one "B" player (or worse) to be on your team if you want to keep your "A" players happy. Because "A" players can't and won't delegate to "B" or "C" players because they can't trust the fact that the work will get done.

In order to provide great advice and service to your clients, it is not enough just for you to be a great Advisor – you also need a great team. In order to build & maintain this great team, you need to create a great culture.

When California imposed the "shelter-in-place" in March of 2020 and everyone on our team was forced to work from home, in the middle of unprecedented market volatility, our firm's culture was put to the test. It would have been understandable and even acceptable by some clients if we were out of communication for a week or more and unable to place trades or handle service items. But none of this occurred, not even for a day. Peter Drucker famously said "Culture eats strategy for breakfast" and those sentiments rang true for our firm as we have never come up with a strategy for "what to do when the world turns upside down."

SECTION IV

DESERVING & EARNING REFERRALS

You Can be Worth $1,000 an Hour

What makes the financial planner profession different than most others is that it comes in many different forms. Some days your job is to be the strategist, some days it's a money manager, some days it's a project manager, and some days it's a marriage counselor. I have some clients who see me consistently as the same thing (i.e. in every meeting I am "the money manager" or "the strategist"). I have other clients where my role varies from day to day. One thing that is common is that I am always the **Chief Problem Solver**.

If a client is financially successful and has enough moving parts in their life, you should be able to create value that is 5 to 10 times the price they are paying you for your services.

10 Habits of Highly Successful Advisors

1. Successful Advisors are committed to lifelong learning. They take learning seriously (i.e., when they attend a conference, they actually attend the meetings, ask questions, take notes.). When they listen to a podcast, they write down 1 or 2 new ideas that they learned, and they keep all of this in their 'ideas journal'.

2. They join best practices groups, and they travel to learn from the best. In my career I've had the privilege of spending a full day with several different multi-million-dollar Wealth Management firms doing nothing but drinking from the fountain of knowledge. Each of these was orchestrated by me simply reaching out and asking and offering to do something in exchange.

3. They find great mentors. My career has been bestowed with more great mentors than you can imagine. All great Advisors that I know can say the same thing about their careers. Find a great mentor.

4. They view their client relationships with a "win-win" or don't play mentality. They are truly committed to serving their clients and not just selling them something.

5. They have great attitudes and are a joy to be around. This makes them attractive and easy to refer to others. That being said, their joy is genuine and so they don't come across as being "salesy".

6. They take Nick Murray's advice and view their client list like Noah's Arc – not enough room for everyone to get on board. If you take on clients that you don't like or genuinely care about it will wear on you over time, rob you of your energy and creative spirit, and

impact the rest of your business. I have what's called the "cell phone rule" that says if I saw this person's name pop up on my cell phone and I didn't want to take the call, don't take them on as a client. (That same token applies to existing clients).

7. They are focused on being effective, not just efficient. Peter Drucker famously said, "Efficiency is doing things right; effectiveness is doing the right things." Successful Advisors are laser focused on doing the things that move the dial in their business. That is why they don't need to work 50-60 hours a week their entire career.

8. They know how to build and manage a team, and they know how to share the rewards with their team. Every great Advisor I know brags about how great their team is.

9. Successful Advisors love mentoring others.

10. Successful Advisors pay it forward. A couple of years ago I was considering adding an options-overlay strategy to our in-house ETF portfolio models. I found an options trader in San Francisco who worked with firms like mine to do this very thing and spent a few hours with him learning more about how this all could work. Then I emailed two legends in our industry, Harold Evensky and Larry Swedroe and asked them what they thought about this idea. Both run firms similar to ours and both have decades of experience managing other people's money. Each one of them responded to my email within 24 hours and were thoughtful and candid in their response. Neither of them knew me or even knew of me. Both were willing to pay it forward and share their thoughts and experience with me.

How to Think About the Profession

As Jim Rohn taught us many years ago, you don't get paid for your time (the hour), you get paid for the value that you bring to the hour.

To illustrate my point, here are some real numbers. If your goal is to produce $1M in recurring revenue each year, and your goal is to work 1,500 hours (30 hours a week with 2 weeks' vacation), you need to generate $666 per hour. Can this be done (without turning into a used car salesman who views clients with dollar signs in their eyes?) – As Jim Rohn would also say, the answer is "of course!"

The way to accomplish this is to work almost exclusively on items that produce economic value for your clients.

To do that, you must do 4 things:

1. Know your client's entire financial situation inside and out

    a. Know what and who is important to them
    b. This means you must collect their tax returns every year and study them
    c. You must know the terms of their debt (interest rate, loan amount, duration, etc.)
    d. You must know where all their assets are held, not just what you manage
    e. You must review all their insurance
    f. You must know about their Social Security, pensions, expected inheritance, etc.

2. Keep abreast of what's going on in the world

   a. Tax laws
   b. Estate planning strategies
   c. Investment strategies
   d. Charitable planning
   e. College planning

3. Stop wasting your time

   a. At my firm, everyone can see everyone else's calendars. This way we don't waste time trying to coordinate internal meetings.
   b. We also don't waste time playing "who's on first" – this is the game that occurs when an Advisor or Principal emails 2 or 3 people asking that a specific task gets done. When that happens, often each person assumes that someone else will handle it and then no one handles it. Leaving the Advisor or Principal to come back and check on said task, only to find out it was never completed.

      i. We had this problem at our firm many years ago and we brought in a Practice Management Consultant to help with this (and a variety of other problems). She said if the last name of the client starts with A-L, assign the task to staff member A. If the last name of the client starts with M-Z, assign the task to staff member B. That simple solution immediately solved our "who's on first" problem.

4. Make Their Problems Your Problems

   a. We live in a world where everyone wants to pass the buck. We get frustrated with large corporations because we can never get ahold of someone who has the power to decide or fix our problem. **This is our opportunity to be different.**

   b. If you build a big enough network and surround yourself with competent professionnals, you'll be amazed at all the wonderful things you can do for your clients.

   c. I've helped clients get job interviews, make professional connections that boosted their careers, and a host of other positives. But I've also helped them when they lost their passport in Europe or had their briefcase stolen when it was full of their confidential financial documents.

If you want to build a loyal client base – make sure your clients know, their problems are your problems.

Good Service vs. Exceptional Client Service

"Good is the enemy of great" – John D. Rockefeller

Every Financial Advisor I know says they provide excellent client service – in fact many even say so on their website.

They will give examples like "I return all calls and emails within 24 hours". Admittedly that is a good standard and one I would advocate, but I would not call that in of itself exceptional client service. The best Financial Advisors can all tell you stories of things we've done to go above and

---

beyond. Helping clients buy cars, writing letters of recommendation for their kids, helping their elderly parents organize their tax documents, etc.

Here is a simple example I can give to help you differentiate between good service and exceptional service.

I had a client recently who wanted to buy a home. We helped him crunch all the numbers in terms of how much home he could afford, what the ideal down payment would be, how to raise the funds in the most tax efficient manner, etc. etc. Then he asked for an introduction to a mortgage broker, which we provided (3 names, I let him pick).

I'd say everything done thus far counts as good client service.

Now to take things to the next level, with his permission, we shared his net worth statement and income projections with the mortgage broker. We determined the optimal mix of down payment vs. loan amount, and the ideal loan terms given his objectives. The mortgage broker then provided a pre-qualification letter (multiple versions with different housing price amounts).

We then connected him with a realtor in the area and provided her everything she would need to help him make an offer. In the meantime we started gathering everything the mortgage broker would need to underwrite his loan so that as soon as his offer was approved the loan processing could begin.

All the client had to do was decide how much of a monthly mortgage he was comfortable with and go look at houses.

And when the client did find the house of his dreams, we helped him with all of the negotiations.

Having bought a home myself recently, this is the type of experience I wish I had someone to help me with.

This business is easy when you treat clients the way you would want to be treated if the roles were reversed.

<u>Final Thought – there are Advisors out there who will say what we did here was a waste of time.</u>

I would counter that this is my marketing plan. I'd rather spend my time jumping through hoops to help an existing client and turn them into a raving fan in the process than take a stranger out to lunch or host a seminar for tire kickers.

Teach, Their Children Well

In 2013 my business partner suggested that we try to forge relationships with all our clients' adult children. We were struggling in the marketing department and his thinking was, our clients were in their 60s and 70s and so their kids were all highly educated, well-paid professionals in their 30's and 40's. We spent the next couple of years reaching out to our clients' adult children (with their parents' permission of course) and managed to get a dozen or so as clients.

For a variety of reasons this effort was less than a smashing success, but one great thing came out of it – **it forced us to figure out how we could help our client's kids.**

Someone once said, **<u>the nicest thing you can do for someone is to do something nice for their children.</u>** As a father of three I can completely relate to this quote and have found it to be very much true in our business.

We started by putting together a 200-page financial literacy course that covers everything from stocks vs. bonds to why you should sign up for your company's 401K plan to how to read your tax return. Nine years and many revisions later, this financial literacy course is still in use today and has been used with many of our client's kids, ranging in age from 15 to 35.

Because of this, we have established ourselves as being there to help however and whenever we can.

We send our client's kids graduation presents when they graduate from High School or College. We send them useful information when we learn that they started a new job. We help them enroll in their benefits plans at work and fill out their W4s.

Not a week goes by that I don't have at least one of my client's kids calling or emailing me and asking me for financial advice. And you know what – I love it. I am happy to help, and I know that this is often the #1 thing I can do to help their parents, my actual clients.

Fast forward to today and many of those same clients who were too young, didn't meet our minimums, or were not serious about planning back in 2013 are now ideal clients. And because their parents have gotten older, we are hosting Family Meetings where we help generation 2 understand all the moving parts and pieces in generation 1's financial life so that they can start to get involved and so that there are no surprises down the road.

Wrapping Up

There is no shortage of things you can read on how to get more referrals. In my career I've seen many different Advisors take many different approaches to this question, all with varying degrees of success. As I've said, I never had great success in obtaining referrals by asking for them (when I did ask, the names I received rarely ended up being the kind of clients I was seeking). All my success in this area has come from deserving referrals and this is the approach I would recommend you take as well.

SECTION V

RUNNING THE WEALTH MANAGEMENT BUSINESS

How to Think About Partnerships

If you build a team, which you must do in order to build a $1M+ recurring revenue firm, at some point you will at least consider the idea of forming a partnership. That word is used loosely in our industry as not all forms of partnership are the same.

In my career I've been a part of every type of partnership you can imagine. I've also managed a lot of Advisors who formed various forms of the following partnerships and I've helped build them and helped transition them when things fell apart.

Let's quickly walk through a few of the forms of partnership FA's can enter into:

1. **Office Space & Staff Partnerships (weak)** – a space partnership is where the only thing the individuals really share is the physical space where they work (and sometimes an admin who does basic service work). My

109

clients are mine, your clients are yours, but we pay for common space. In this type of partnership, I can use whatever software I want, manage investments however I want, etc. You can of course do the same and while we might collaborate and commiserate, we are not bound by one another's decisions. Finally, we can and often do each market our practices differently and with separate names (Smith Financial vs. The Jones Financial Group). This is the exact type of arrangement you would see at most Wire House firms.

2. **Client Partnerships (strong)** – in this form of partnership we share some, if not all of the clients. An example here could be, I'm good at bringing in new clients but you're really good at financial planning. So, I do all the marketing and you manage the actual relationship, do the planning, etc. We split the revenue 50/50. This type of partnership includes everything in the Office Space & Staff partnership + now we are also sharing clients. I've seen other examples where one Advisor loves investments and the other one loves insurance, so Advisor A sits in all investment related meetings, answers all investment related emails, etc. whereas Advisor B only participates in the Insurance meetings, only answers insurance related emails. The revenue split for this type of arrangement is much harder because investment management pays a small amount every year whereas an insurance product often pays a large amount but only periodically. This

is the exact type of arrangement you would see at independent broker-dealers and insurance owned broker-dealers.

3. **Revenue Partnerships (strongest)** – also known as an Ensemble firm. This is the type of partnership I have today, and it includes everything mentioned in the first two types of partnership plus includes actual sharing of all revenue. For example, in our firm every cent that comes in goes into a bank account owned by the company. As owners/partners, we collect a salary just like everyone else but since we are an S corp., at the end of the year we get a K1 that says what our share of the profits are. We take money out of the bank account in proportion to our ownership to both cover taxes and of course earn profits for being the owners of the business. This is the exact type of arrangement you would see at RIAs and Wealth Management firms.

Every form of partnership has its pros and cons and there is no panacea. With the first firm of partnership, breaking up is easy to do but there are few economies of scale. With the second form of partnership, the marketing is easier to do but complications still arise because every piece of business has a different split and feelings are often hurt because compensation is a constant discussion item.

The third form of partnership is the hardest to unwind (it's basically a divorce for a business) but also creates a true team environment. Everyone is part of the same team with the same marketing plan, the same goals, and a shared set of clients.

My advice in this area is to go slowly, much like going from dating to marriage. A normal progression would be to go from dating to moving in together to marriage. I would advise a similar progression through the various forms of partnerships. **My other piece of advice is to write up an agreement in advance that spells out what will happen if the partnership gets dissolved.**

Why Succession Planning is Harder Than You Think

In 2010, I was up in Alaska visiting some Advisors that were part of my territory because there was a problem. "Jim" had convinced his daughter's husband "Matt" to quit his job and join the company so he could take over Jim's business. Matt was to train under Jim for 2 years, taking a drastic pay cut in the process, and then take over and buy Jim out over 5 years at which point his income would exceed anything he has previously imagined.

Three years in and Jim thought things were going great. So great in fact, he said he was working less and making more than ever before. In fact, now he was so happy that he decided to postpone the buyout for 5 more years…

Matt was not happy. He had spent the past 3 years doing everything Jim had asked, added all sorts of systems and processes to the business, and taken over a bunch of client relationships. In fact, he had made the business more valuable which would now work against his favor as the actual buyout terms hadn't been agreed to yet.

I wish I could say this was a unique story but it's not – in fact in my experience this is more the rule than the exception. In fact, in 2014 when I was in a similar position, nearly the exact same thing happened to me. The person I was supposed to buy the business from tried to push back the purchase date and increase the purchase price because like Jim, he was working less and making more because I was working more and making less.

In both Jim/Matt's case and in my case, I was able to work things out and create a win-win outcome. However, that's not always the case and our industry is full of examples where things didn't work out and both sides were forced to start over.

I was recently asked by a new Advisor who was about to buy a practice how to avoid this exact same scenario.

I gave him the following advice:

- Talk to the retiring Advisor about this risk upfront. Tell them this stuff happens all the time and you want to proactively address it vs. ignoring this risk and assuming "it won't happen to you".
- Get a contract written as soon as reasonable that outlines the terms, to include the date and purchase price.
- Include a clause that either gives the seller an incentive to adhere to the original date or a punishment for pushing back said date.
- Meet weekly and talk about what is happening, how the transition is going, how you feel about it, etc.

The #1 reason this stuff falls apart is because the seller's "why" for retiring isn't big enough. When the markets are volatile and the phone's ringing off the hook, a lot of Advisors are "ready to sell and retire". Then things calm down, their Jr. Advisor picks up a bunch of slack, the market rallies and they forget why they wanted to retire in the first place. Start by really understanding their 'Why' and, ask them what they plan to do once they retire. This business is hard to retire from and that is why a lot of Advisors sell and stay.

Living Your Best Life

"The things you own end up owning you" – Tyler Durden in Fight Club

I've started this section off with this quote because while it was initially meant to describe physical 'things' like cars and furniture, it's also a great description for how most business owners feel. In fact, there is an entire industry of consultants who exist to teach successful business owners how to delegate more responsibility inside of their firm so they can take more vacation days.

Early in my career I was mentored by four very successful Advisors, and they taught me a ton, some directly and some indirectly. One of the lessons all four of them taught me was that once their business reached a certain level of financial success, they lost control of their time.

Witnessing this, I decided early in my career to never let this happen to me. Thinking back to the 3 I's and what attracted me to this profession in the first place, I wanted my independence. I wanted it because I knew someday I would want to be a very involved father (and I am proud to say that I coach both my son's little league teams, take them to and from school, and never miss the important events in their lives). I wanted it because I knew that life was short, and a healthy retirement is not guaranteed. And I wanted it because, I figured if I was going to take all the risk and stress that comes with owning your own business, then I should at least be able to control my own schedule.

Here are a few pointers for ensuring that the thing you own doesn't end up owning you:

- Don't convince people they need what you are offering – either someone inherently gets it, or they don't. We can talk DIYers into hiring us, but we are only setting ourselves up for disaster and heartache down the road.
- Only hire "A" players and pay them very well.
  - Two "A" players is better than two "B's" and two "C's" for the same price.
    - This seems obvious but I've heard advisors say "I want a bigger staff so that I have overlap and backup in case someone is sick or quits."
- Don't take on bad clients and if you do by accident, abort ship once you figure out that they are not a fit.
- Think like a dentist – at the end of a meeting agenda, under next steps, state clearly when this person should expect to meet with you again.

- Learn from Dan Sullivan – Founder of the Strategic Coach, Dan teaches about focus days, buffer days and free days.

  o A focus day is when you are meeting with clients and producing revenue.

  o A buffer day is when you are preparing for client meetings or doing follow up after client meetings.

  o A free day means you are not working at all. A free day could be a Saturday or a Sunday which may seem obvious but that means no checking email! The idea behind a free day is that you are not only not working but also not thinking about work! *Easier said than done I know.*

- Early in my career I would meet with anyone, anywhere, anytime. I had some clients who lived 2+ hours away and I'd drive to see them for each meeting. I had one client who only wanted to meet on Friday nights from 6-8pm. We did this about once a month for a year.

- Over time I changed this but not in one fell swoop. First, I started telling clients we really needed to meet in my office because in our conference room we have a large monitor and I can project all of their financial information and make updates in real time. This worked because it was true and once clients started coming in and seeing how much more effective these meetings were, the issue of where we should meet never came up again.

116

- Then, when I was scheduling meetings, I stopped offering Mondays or Fridays as an option. I decided to follow the Dan Sullivan method and make those buffer days, with Tuesday-Thursday focus days. I've found this system really works for me because on Mondays I can prepare for what's coming and on Friday's I can send clients my post meeting summaries & action items. This also made me enjoy my Sundays more because I knew I didn't have to worry about whether I was fully prepared for a client meeting the following day.

- Finally, I decided that I would only conduct client meetings between 9am and 2pm on Tuesdays, Wednesdays, and Thursdays. I've found that I am better in the morning and clients deserve to get advice from me when I am at my best.

- This means when I offer a client some dates for a meeting, they are during my ideal times. That being said, once every couple of weeks I will have a client that needs to talk about something urgently and can only talk on a Monday, a Friday or in the afternoon. This is not a hill I am willing to die on, so of course I will make that accommodation.

I recommend reading the e-Myth by Michael Gerber to better understand this concept. Small business ownership can be a great path to generational wealth and independence, but it can also be a low wage job if you lose control over your time.

Parting Ways with Difficult Clients

One of the biggest areas I see younger/newer Advisors struggle with is when to part ways with a difficult client.

For the actual verbiage on how to do it, look at Nick Murray's book titled *Scripts*, he has a specific one dedicated just to this topic.

In general, I think there are 3 main reasons to part ways with a client:

1. You don't like them and therefore your heart isn't into helping them as best you can
2. They are rude to your staff
3. They want something you cannot deliver. The best example being market timing or a client that thinks you should be able to match the stock market in up years without commensurate performance in the down years.

Because we tend to obtain clients via referrals from existing clients or COIs, it's never easy to part ways with a client for fear there will be a ripple effect. Nowadays you also have to worry about negative google or social media reviews, so it's very important to part ways amicably.

Regardless of why you are parting ways with the client, I think it's best to make it seem as though you are doing them a favor as opposed to punishing them. For me that sounds something like:

"I am concerned that I may not be able to match your expectations as far as what a Financial Advisor can provide. Over the past few (*insert time period*), our emails and conversations have led me to understand better what you are seeking, and my experience tells me this is not something I/we are suited for. I think in fairness to you its best that we part ways, effective at the end of this month. I will resign from managing your accounts and stop billing you completely, though your accounts will remain with (XYZ custodian) and your access to them will not be impacted. If you would like some recommendations on other Advisors to interview, let me know. I have enjoyed working with you and wish you and your family the best."

How to Structure Your Time

Building and maintaining a $1M+ of recurring revenue might require you to think about your time a little differently than you do today. Here's how I think about my time:

- I want to work no more than 30 hours per week (this excludes time spent reading outside the office).
- I want to take 4 weeks of vacation per year (for me that's a week around the 4th of July, a week for Thanksgiving and 2 weeks between Christmas and New Year's).
- I want to produce at least $1M of recurring revenue per year.
- If I work 30 hours per week, 48 weeks per year, my total hours worked = 1,440 hours per year.
- If I divide $1,000,000 by 1,440, that means I need to produce revenue at a rate of $694 per hour.

Knowing this is my minimum revenue needed per hour (and as I've said in the introduction, my personal number is much higher than this), there are only 5 things you can do that are worth $694 per hour.

Make note of these items and when you catch yourself doing something that is not on the list, figure out why you are doing it and who on your team should be doing it from now on:

1. Meet with Clients
2. Meet with pre-screened Prospective Clients
3. Sharpen the Saw (yes, reading can be a $1K per hour activity)
4. Manage and mentor your team members
5. Manage the business

For all of this to work, you have to realize that time is your greatest asset and manage your time wisely. Here is a system that I have developed over the years and has worked for me:

How to Structure Your Year

- Start each new year by taking an inventory of your client base (get very specific, include name, age, assets with you, recurring revenue, etc.) as this is your number 1 asset and a good place to start your planning.
- Write out your business plan. I've written out a business plan every year that I've been in this profession and will continue to do so every year until I retire. After the business plan is written I present it to my team and my business coach for feedback. I also share it with a few other peer Advisors and receive theirs in return.

- Develop an annual calendar so you can plan for when you will have heavy client periods vs. light client periods (for us mid Jan through early May is busy, then September through year-end is busy). This will allow you to think about when you will attend conferences, when you will take vacation, and when you can realistically fit in any new ventures you are working on this year.

How to Structure Your Quarter

- Review your business plan with your team, identify what has and hasn't worked and make course corrections before another quarter passes you by. Review all KPIs with the team.
- Identify specific projects you either personally want to get done or want your team to get done in the next 90 days.

* Key Performance Indicators (KPIs)

The health of a business can be measured using a few KPIs. The balance here is that on the one hand you can identify a dozen important metrics to measure. And on the other hand, you can't forget to "make the main thing the main thing." Given that, we've settled on 5 KPIs by which to measure the health of our business:

1. **Total Revenue** – this is the actual revenue that will show up on our tax return, not 'GDC' for those of you working in a wire house.

2. **New Assets Under Management** - this is new money coming in, it does not factor in performance, and we do not subtract from this number when a client makes a large withdrawal. The reason being is that the client saved and invested their money for a reason, and I don't want anyone to feel like our firm is not in favor of clients deciding to make a withdrawal so they can spend and enjoy some of that savings.

3. **Points for Net New Clients** – Years ago we measured simply, clients in and clients out. At the end of the year, we netted these two numbers out and reported that we added X # of new clients to our roster. But then one day it hit me, adding a platinum client is obviously quite different from adding a bronze client, but more importantly, losing a platinum client is much worse than losing a bronze client! That day we developed a points system, which works as follows:

   a. A new client added is worth either 1, 2, 3, or 4 points (depending upon the revenue level).

   b. A client lost is worth 1, 2, 3, or 4 points (depending upon the revenue level).

   c. If for example we add one platinum client (4 points) and lose 2 bronze clients (1 point each), we'd be at net +2, even though our total client count went down.

   d. This may seem obvious, but the goal is to work with fewer clients that want deeper, more robust relationships with us vs. having lots of surface level relationships.

4. **Referrals & Leads** – this one is pretty self-explanatory; we track every referral we receive, even if it's just a client saying, "I want you to know I gave your name to my friend, Joe Smith". Regardless of whether or not we ever hear from Joe, his name and the name of the referral go on our spreadsheet. Passive referrals are an indication that our existing clients are pleased with our work and that we are referrable. Leads are an indication that our name has some standing in the community and/or our website and SEO are paying dividends.

5. **Client Meetings** – Everyone at the firm can see everyone else's calendar. We color code all meetings with yellow for prospects and red for clients. At the end of each month, we track how many total client meetings were held, and how many were held by each Advisor. Client meetings are the key to 3 things:

   a. High retention of existing clients
   b. Identifying opportunities for new assets to manage
   c. Obtaining passive referrals

How to Structure Your Month

There are 3 non-client focused thing I know I will have on my calendar each month.

1. Monthly Investment Committee Meetings – topics vary by month; agenda is sent in advance. We cover

everything from market & economic updates to portfolio performance for the month and year-to-date.

2. A rotating series of staff meetings
3. A review of the firm's financials.

A deep dive into how we conduct our investment committee meetings is beyond the scope of this book. But I will give some insight into how we conduct our staff meetings and how I recommend reviewing your firm's financials.

Weekly Agenda/Staff meeting

I've been a part of a lot of different teams, some tried a daily meeting, others monthly. **I have found that a weekly team meeting is the right frequency.**

At our firm we meet for 60 minutes every Wednesday, and we rotate the topics by week. We have a 1st Wednesday agenda, a 2nd Wednesday agenda, etc. The wild card is the occasional month where there is a 5th Wednesday, and we use that for "open topics". If our meeting lasts 35 minutes on any given week and no one has anything else to share, the meeting is over. Meaning we block 60 minutes but the culture at our firm is such that we don't like sitting in meetings, everyone has work to do and the meeting exists as a form of communication. Once the communication has been made, the meeting can end early.

Here are some example topics:

1st Wednesday:

- Leads & Referrals
- New client onboarding
- Life insurance illustrations – to be requested

2nd Wednesday:

- New opportunities
- Financial Planning update

3rd Wednesday:

- Client Appointment Calendar
- Life insurance illustrations – to be reviewed
- Tax update

4th Wednesday:

- Licensing (people moved out of state / deaths / change of trustee)
- Compliance update

Review Monthly financials

Every month we update our P&L, our Balance Sheet, and our Cash Flow Projections (CFP) worksheet. While I love the P&L and encourage every business owner to review theirs with a fine-tooth comb, the P&L tells you what already happened. Therefore, we also use a Cash Flow Projection, which is always run for the balance of the calendar year, to show what we expect to happen. The CFP is simple, it shows current money in the bank + expected recurring revenue + expected one-time revenue less expected expenses = cash in the bank. Early in my career these numbers were scary as they would show "come

September we have a problem". Now our recurring revenue far exceeds our expenses, and any one-time revenue becomes the cherry on top. But this is still useful because if I want to give a staff member a large one-time bonus as an example or make a shareholder's distribution, the CFP can model the impact of either of these plus a host of others.

A few other thoughts on the firm's financials:

- Spend 1 hour a month reviewing these no matter what.
- Occasionally pick an expense and ask to see the details. If I see that our internet/telephone bill which is usually $600/mo. was $800 last month, I want to know why and I want to see it with my own eyes. I am fortunate that my wife does all the books for both of my firms, but you may not be so lucky, and this wasn't always the case for me. Stories of bookkeepers stealing a little bit of money at a time for many years are abundant. Plus, you might be getting ripped off by one of your service providers and not even be aware of it. Double billings happen all the time since most invoices just get paid without question.
- Only Allow Positive Surprises - Be conservative with your estimates. Overestimate your expenses and underestimate your projected income. Markets decline, clients die, life insurance policies don't get placed, you get the idea. I want to be prepared for the worst-case financial scenario and then pleasantly surprised by the actual results.

- Once a quarter compare your revenue & expenses, by category, to your estimates from your CFP. This will then show you the variance by line item and you can home in on where your assumptions are missing the mark.
- Set aside 40% of your profits for taxes. Remember you should be receiving a W2 salary where taxes are automatically withheld, and a share of profits in proportion to your ownership. Each time you take a shareholder's distribution you need to set aside 40% for taxes. Pay your estimated taxes out of this pool of funds and sit on the rest. Come April if it turns out you don't owe the full 40%, you now have extra money you can move into your vacation fund.

How to Structure Your Week

- I mentioned earlier that I use the Dan Sullivan strategic coach model (focus, buffer and free days mentioned earlier)
  - Reserve Mondays & Fridays for administrative tasks (compliance, booking travel), preparing for client meetings, business planning, attending Webinars (sharpening the saw), and having lunch with COIs.
  - Tues-Thurs – time on stage. 2-3 client meetings per day, calls in between.
- Start your week by making a list of goals/tasks for the week = 1st thing I do on Monday morning, add to it

throughout the week, last thing I review before I leave on Friday.

- Before your week is over, check for any emails that have a red-flag next to them and see if they can be addressed before you leave for the weekend.

How to Conduct Effective One-on-One's with your team

I have a weekly 1-1 lasting 30 minutes with almost every member of my team. All non-revenue producing staff meet with me weekly, as does my business Partner. Revenue-producing team members meet with me on an as needed basis. Their time is valuable, as is mine, and shooting the proverbial 'you know what' for an hour each week is an expensive proposition. For non-revenue producing team members, this is how I manage them effectively and ensure they are working on the right projects. Because everyone on our team is truly an "A" player this is not micromanaging on my part but rather our chance to check in and confirm what is important. Remember, some tasks are urgent, some tasks are important, some tasks are both and some are neither. I want my staff working on the things that are most important to the firm, even if they are not urgent. We use a web-based software called SmartQ to track every task/ project being worked on. This software allows you to create one dashboard per person and physically move tasks along a virtual assembly line. Each task is a little bubble where the subject is visible but then you can click on it to see the details. <u>I cannot recommend this software highly enough.</u> When one of our team members went out on paternity leave 2 weeks earlier than expected, we knew exactly what he was working on and where he was at with each project.

128

How to Structure Your Day

- My calendar is pre-populated with all my client's birthdays. I call or email clients on their birthday depending on the relationship.
- I then start by reviewing all emails that have arrived since I left the previous day and I either handle them or delegate them.
- I "red-flag" emails that come in throughout the day that cannot be fully addressed (I may even send a recognition response, flag, then fully respond).
- At the end of the day before leaving, I quickly scan any "red-flagged" emails to see if they have been addressed or can be addressed before I go.

Managing Your Time & Staying Organized:

- Emails vs. Phone Calls – there's a bit of an art that comes with knowing when to handle something via email vs. over the phone. Some of it has to do with the client, some of it has to do with the subject matter, and some of it has to do with the situation (who reached out to who). As an example, the other day a client sent me an email asking 4 questions about his annuity. Two of his questions were easy and straight-forward and could have been answered via email, but the other two were complex. My thought was that answering those complex questions via email would have led to him: A. responding with another email which then would have led me to write him back and possibly started an email chain, and B. might not have been clear enough to address his question. Part of email correspondence is understanding what's really at the heart of the matter, which may not be apparent from the questions themselves. In this situation I responded something like "these are great questions, of all which I am happy to address; I will call you in an hour." The entire conversation took less than 30 minutes, and all his questions were addressed.

- Managing Your Week – On Monday morning I look at all my meetings that are scheduled for the week ahead, plus the emails that I've received since leaving on Friday, plus any emails I flagged (more on this) from the previous week. I then make a written to-do list for the week. That list is with me until every item gets checked off.

- Managing Your Inbox – When an important email comes in, I flag it in red. Even if I am planning to address it immediately or forward it to a colleague, I flag it. I do this for two reasons:

  o I might be halfway through it and a co-worker walks into my office or the phone rings and now I'm distracted.

  o It helps me later quickly scan through my inbox and identify the important emails that deserve a 2nd look. Let's say a client emails me and says, "I need a $10K withdrawal from my Schwab account". I will flag that email and forward it to Geoff. Even though I'm 99% sure Geoff will handle it without any further direction from me, later in the day or week when I'm scrolling through my red-flagged emails, I will log into Schwab and check the client's transaction history to confirm that the $10K went out. If it did, the email gets unflagged and I move on. If it hasn't, I contact Geoff to see what happened.

- o At the end of every day before I "finish", I check all my flagged emails to make sure everything is either done or in process.
- o Even if an item cannot be handled immediately, the client will receive an email letting them know that we are "on it." All emails are responded to within 24 hours and all calls are returned same day. It's extremely important to let your entire team know that this is the expectation at your office. Even if the email response is simply to say – I've received your email and we are working on it, expect to hear back from me or "Geoff/Jennifer/Ryan" in the next 2-3 days.

- My Giant White Board – I have a white board in my office that is probably 10 feet wide and 5 feet long. Its divided into 3 categories – left side is opportunities I am working on, middle is client service and planning, and the right hand side is larger business planning items. The goal of the white board is not to capture things that can be dealt with that day. These are reserved for projects or tasks that take weeks, or sometimes months to finish.

If you don't have a system for managing your time, you will always feel behind and you will end up working nights and weekends to catch up.

How to Take a Global View of the Business

Over the years my co-workers have joked that I have "a spreadsheet for everything" and that is absolutely true. The reason is because, while at the client level you need to understand their unique situation, you also must maintain a global view of the business.

How many households are you managing, how many investment accounts, how many have insurance products where you are listed as the servicing agent, etc.

Here are some examples that I would suggest you create as well:

- Annuities – Even though each client's annuity would be listed in their personal financial plan, we also have a Master Annuity spreadsheet that lists every annuity across all clients where I am the Servicing Advisor. This is sorted by Insurance Company and includes every field imaginable, including when we plan to turn on the lifetime income rider. This way at the beginning of each year we can scan this spreadsheet and quickly see who we need to prepare paperwork for and start having those discussions with the client. Sidebar – if a client has been taking systematic withdrawals from their Schwab account, we will advise them that once their annuity is turned on, that we plan to reduce the amount of their Schwab withdrawals by a commensurate amount unless they tell us otherwise.

- Life & Disability Insurance – Again, even though each client's insurance policies would be listed on their personal financial plan, we also have a Master Insurance spreadsheet that lists every policy across all clients where I am the Advisor listed. This would include the policy anniversary date and is sorted by that vs. the insurance company. For permanent life policies, this report is run on a monthly basis so we know when its time to request an annual mid-stream or "in-force" illustration. For term policies, this report alerts us to when a policy may be coming to the end of its term (i.e. 10 year policy bought in June of 2013). This way we can start having that conversation with the client.
- Client Appointment Calendar – This gets downloaded from our CRM each month and this is where we track the client levels and the frequency with which we plan to meet with each client. This spreadsheet tells us who is "due" for a check-in within the next 30 days.
- Mortgages – Again, each client's mortgage would be a part of their personal financial plan, but the master spreadsheet allows us to take a firm-level view and see who should be looking at a refinance based on current rates.
- Leads & Referrals – We track every lead (SEO, inbound inquiry) and every referral we receive. This is true even for the ones where a client says, "I want you to know I referred my sister Betty to you" and Betty never contacted us. Why track these? I believe that if we are doing a great job for our clients, we should be

getting referrals without asking. In fact, I don't believe in asking for referrals and covered that in the marketing section of the book. We have found that on average we receive about 40 referrals per year. My former colleague Karl Brantley up in Eugene Oregon was the best Advisor I've ever known in terms of receiving unsolicited referrals – he averaged about 60 per year in the time we worked together. The reason for Karl's success in this area was simple – he was an expert in the Oregon PERS system and all his clients knew this. As a result, whenever someone in their circle asked a question about PERS they would get referred to Karl. Having this spreadsheet helps us see our potential pipeline of new clients, tells us if we are doing a great job for our existing clients, and reminds us of who we need to reach out to.

- New Business Opportunities – Once a month during our weekly staff meeting, we review our new business opportunities. These are not pie in the sky but rather things that have been presented to the client and have a 90%+ chance of moving forward. Items included would be a new client that has signed a financial planning agreement, an existing client who is rolling over a new account, a new life insurance policy a client is purchasing through us, etc. There are several reasons we track these items:

- It gets the entire team on the same page and avoids the silos that naturally come up in an ensemble firm like ours.
- It gently reminds all the revenue producing team members that we can't rest on our laurels. If you know that you are doing a great job for your clients and always acting in a fiduciary capacity, you should never be bashful about the fact that your recommendations are being implemented. If a client wants help with estate tax planning, I will show them several ways to tackle that issue. One of them will be using an ILIT and will include a life insurance policy with me acting as the Agent. If that's the best thing for the client, then that's what you should do. And then that opportunity becomes listed on our new business spreadsheet.
- It helps populate our cash flow projection as potential expected revenue.

How to Think About Firm Profitability - 65/15/20

You must build a world-class team to provide excellent advice and service to your clients.

Your world class team is not going to come cheap, nor would you want it to because then it wouldn't be sustainable.

The question then becomes, how do you build something great but also make sure that that same great team won't become a financial anchor if & when the firm's revenue declines.

Some firms never build the all-star team they should because they fear having high fixed costs matched up against a declining revenue base. This is the equivalent of the investor who never has enough exposure to equities because of the fear that they might temporarily decline. In 2008 many RIAs had to engage in layoffs for this very reason. Coming out of 2009 they were slow to rehire. Being under-staffed or having "C" players on the team because they don't command higher salaries is not the right way to address this concern.

To avoid all of this, I suggest a 65/15/20 framework, which is as follows:

- Allocate 65% of revenues to Principals & Staff costs. This includes salaries, bonuses, and benefits. This would not include any profits. All team members (including the owners/partners) should be paid a salary.
    - Admittedly establishing a salary for Principals is more difficult than it is for staff because Principals tend to have 2 or 3 roles within the firm. That being said, the annual compensation surveys mentioned earlier in the book are a good starting place for determining what these numbers should be.
- Allocate 15% of revenues to overhead costs. This includes rent, software, marketing, etc.
- This leaves a 20% profit margin. Profits should be shared proportionately with owners. For example, a

Partner in a firm may get a 50% of revenue draw/salary + benefits + a year-end bonus + a share of profits. A non-Partner Advisor might have the same compensation structure but without the share of profits.

Within your 65% allocation, this should be broken further into 2 parts.

- Revenue producing team members – compensation should be entirely revenue based so that as revenue increases, compensation increases. Conversely, if revenue declines, no arbitrary pay cuts are required as compensation will naturally adjust.
- Non-revenue producing team members – In our opinion this should be 75% fixed compensation and 25% variable.

This way in the event of a market/revenue decline, you have a few buffers in place that can help you keep your team without going into debt or tapping into savings.

First, you have a 20% allowance for reduced profits because you are operating at a 20% profit margin and as the owner/partner, your compensation is both your salary (which should be at fair market value) + your share of the profits. You must be able to live off your salary for this to work.

Your second buffer comes from the fact that your biggest expense (compensation to Revenue producing team members) is on a sliding scale based on revenue. So as revenue declines so does their income which helps reduce your expenses. The 3rd buffer comes from the fact that your non-revenue producing staff gets paid 25% variable compensation tied to revenue.

In the event of a March 2020 scenario, you will be able to (and should) tell your entire team that you can get through this without layoffs and that everyone can relax and focus on getting their work done without worrying that they should be looking for a job.

If you have a team in place, go through your P&L and code every category as a #1 or a #2. #1 is all costs related to the team, #2 is all non-team member costs. See how close you are right now to the 65/15/20 allocation model.

Wrapping Up / The Secret Sauce

After 17+ years in the business I'm afraid to say there is no secret sauce. If there is, as they say "its dressed up in overalls and looks like hard work". Like most things in life worth having, there are no shortcuts. But I can give you a few easy things to remember that will certainly help you on your journey:

- Honest intelligent effort is always rewarded.... Eventually.
- The better your team the easier all of this will be, but that costs money.
- Recurring revenue makes the cost of running this whole operation less scary.
- Recurring revenue requires the ability to **add value and deliver on promises**.

- Adding value means you are always sharpening the saw.
- Figure out a way to deliver on your promises and you will build a loyal base of clients which will lead to referrals which all leads to a healthy, growing and thriving business.

If this all sounds difficult, let's compare it with the alternative:

Driving to see clients / Meeting with clients at their houses or worse, Starbucks	Client meetings in my office or via zoom
Meeting with clients at all hours	Meetings are held Tues-Thurs between 9am and 2pm
Meeting with prospective clients that are just tire kickers	Prospective clients are referral only or strongly pre-screened (website has a specific section on costs and minimums)
Meeting with prospective clients that want you to just invest some of their money and then will "see how it goes"	Prospective clients are told in meeting 1 it's a fee + a min AUM and both are firm (AUM varies by Age)
Conducting workshops/seminars	Reading
Dealing with staff turnover because your staff is underpaid and unprofessional	Weekly 1-1 with highly competent staff that prefer autonomy and don't mind being held accountable
Dealing with drama because your staff is underpaid and unprofessional	Over-compensating staff because the firm is growing and they are a huge part of that success

CONCLUSION

My business coach, friend and mentor, Nick Horn recently suggested that I listen to a podcast with Bert Thornton on **High Impact Mentoring** (which is also the name of his most recent book). Bert is the former President and COO of Waffle House and just a few minutes into the interview, I knew exactly why Nick had suggested this podcast. The subtitle of Bert's latest book is "A Practical Guide to Creating Value in Other People's Lives". In Bert's world that was done through hiring, training, and promoting employees at the Waffle House. Throughout the book Bert peppers in stories about individual achievers who started as dishwashers or busboys and by the end of their career were multi-million-dollar franchisees or executives. Bert takes great pride in the fact that his leadership techniques, no doubt, created value in other people's lives.

This concept resonated with me and should resonate with you because that is exactly what we, as Financial Advisors, have the power to do – for our clients, our employees, and those in the industry that we mentor. <u>You can create value in other people's lives and not many people can say that.</u>

As you conclude this book, and hopefully by now this book is filled with highlights, notes, and dog-eared pages, **I encourage you to put these ideas into practice knowing that the rewards will be worth the effort.**

I sign off by including some interesting mini-case studies and anecdotes I hope you find helpful in your journey.

MINI CASE STUDIES & ANECDOTES

Case Study – Positive Impact

In May of 2013 I decided to buy a small tax practice. I talked about this earlier in the book but one of the reasons I bought this practice was to have a captive source of referrals. Things didn't exactly pan out as hoped but in June of 2014 I did receive the perfect referral from the tax practice.

Sheila had lost her husband to a heart attack at just 60 years old, and she didn't know where to turn. They owned a family business and her husband had both run the business and handled the finances for their household. Her first call was to her CPA as she figured he would know where to start. Though he didn't know the 1st thing about postmortem planning (or financial planning) he at least knew enough to send her my way.

While this section is called "the good" I recognize that it's never good when someone dies prematurely. But it does happen and it's one of the times when we as financial planners can step in and add a ton of value to someone's situation. This was exactly one of those scenarios.

What made this set up so perfect for the work that real financial planners do is that it had a little bit of everything, and investments were just part of the equation. The business was a C corp. which owned a life insurance policy on the now deceased. Sheila inherited all the stock in the C corp.

when her husband died, she had no interest in keeping the business. The business had 2 locations and Sheila and her husband owned the land (personally, not in an LLC) that the two locations sat on, and rent was paid to them from the C corp.

This case took two years from start to finish during which time we settled the estate (with a 706 to capture portability), received a step up in basis on the stock so it could then be sold tax free to the buyer, who we helped find. We structured the sale, so Sheila received cash for her stock + guaranteed rent for 10 years + a consulting agreement for 10 years that also allowed her to participate in the employer health insurance plan and the 401K plan until she reached Medicare eligibility. We also got a step up in basis on all four pieces of real estate they owned which allowed Sheila to begin re-depreciating the two rental properties which significantly improved her cash flow.

We consolidated all her assets and used part of the life insurance proceeds to purchase a deferred annuity which will accumulate until her consulting agreement ends, at which point her guaranteed income from the annuity will replace her lost consulting agreement income.

Sheila is still a client today and in the interim period we continue to meet with her each quarter where she updates us on her world travels and we update her on all things financial, estate and tax related. She recently wrote me a letter which I have displayed prominently in my office, where she talked about the impact I've had on her since the untimely passing of her husband. The letter nearly brought tears to my eyes and is something I will cherish for the rest of my life.

Case Study – Sometimes You Can't Win

Gerald called me in early 2011 and said his wife's sister had referred him to me. He told me that a big Wirehouse was managing his money but that his account was small and therefore he didn't get a lot of attention. He wasn't unhappy with his performance; he just needed more planning and attention than what he was receiving. I asked him to send me a recent account statement and after a quick review, told him I would make very little changes to his account if I managed it, but would include financial planning in my standard 1% fee (at the time I was only charging an upfront planning fee, not an ongoing one for clients in his situation).

Gerald said he appreciated my honesty and said he wanted to move his account over immediately.

I don't remember the exact amount, but I recall that it was small, less than $200,000, which was still quite a bit considering that he was in his early 30s and was a CPA (of all things) making roughly $100,000 a year. Now that may be a lot of money in some parts of the country but in the Bay Area, it's just above the poverty line.

Over the next eight years Gerald got married, had 2 kids, and as you can imagine, leaned on us for every single financial decision along the way. We helped him establish life & disability insurance policies, dollar cost average into the market every month, select his and his spouse's employee benefits, create, and implement an estate plan, establish 529 savings accounts, select the right mortgage for each of his home purchases, etc. In fact, at one point, we even helped design his mom's estate plan (she was a widow) because her plan of course would impact him.

By 2019 Gerald's portfolio with our firm had grown to $1,200,000 which was a result of good investment results, account consolidation over time, and a robust savings program we helped initiate.

Out of the blue one-day Gerald emailed my assistant and asked what he had paid last year in total fees to our firm. Given that he was a CPA who completed his own tax returns, my assistant didn't think anything of this question and promptly responded. I however smelled that something was awry and so I reached out to Gerald and asked if he could come in for a review. He responded by asking me the following:

- What has been my performance over the past 5 years and how has that compared to the S&P 500 (for reference, Gerald scored a 50 out of 100 each year on his risk tolerance questionnaire)
- What fees had he paid in total since we began working together

Though I did answer each of his questions (while also pointing out that his benchmark was the required rate of return in his financial plan (<6%) and not the S&P 500 and that he was handsomely beating his personal benchmark), I emphasized that after 8 years of working together this was a conversation that needed to be had in person, not via email.

Gerald responded that he had been meaning to call me but since taking his new job that he just didn't have the time....And then one day he called. He was clearly nervous, and it sounded like he was reading from a script. I don't remember all the details, but he basically said now that I had done all of the heavy lifting with his planning and that the S&P 500 was performing so well, he didn't see the need to pay me each year for my services and would begin managing his investments himself. He went on to say that if he needed some planning work done or a question answered he would reach out and we could come up with a fair arrangement at that time. I responded that under no circumstances would that happen and that after all I had done for him and his family. I delinked his accounts from my institutional master that day and never heard from him again.

Case Study – Document the Important Stuff

In June of 2017 my custodian called me and asked if I would be interested in a partial book of business sale. The Advisor was an investments-only guy who worked from home and conducted his client meetings at his kitchen table. After years of underperformance, he had had enough and was ready to sell all but his 5 best clients. Because his house/office was walking distance from my office, it seemed like a good fit.

He and I met several times to discuss everything from what he was looking for in a successor to what he felt the book of business was worth. We eventually settled on deal terms, and I began meeting with clients and pouring over their investment account statements.

As I met with each of these clients for the 1st time (and the seller sat in each of these initial meetings) it was clear that the performance had been even worse than I had imagined. We aren't talking about underperforming an index, we are talking about losing 30% in 3 years while the index was up 30% during the same 3-year period. And the worst part is that for many of these folks this was their entire life savings.

One lady was reluctant to transfer her account over from the seller to me but eventually did. Let's call her Kari. Kari was a widow when she met the seller and was still working full time as a nurse. The money she had invested was everything she had received from the life insurance when her husband died ($500K). By the time I met her the account was down to $320K between awful performance and a few withdrawals.

I took her through my normal financial planning process and at the end concluded that we should sell everything she owned and invest the proceeds into a globally diversified balanced portfolio. I presented this to her in person, had her sign what we call our "Exhibit A - Investment Mandate" document and sent her an email outlining everything and saying nothing would happen until she approved in writing. She wrote back and said she was nervous but agreed with my recommendations.

Over the next 18 months every call and email I sent her way was ignored on her part. Then one day out of the blue I get an email from a former SEC securities attorney who was now in private practice. He asked me for my entire file on her and said she would be filing an arbitration claim against me and my firm for her investment losses. I forwarded the note to the seller and reminded him that our asset purchase agreement included an indemnification clause that said if I had to pay for any actions he caused, I would be reimbursed by him including my attorneys and accountants' fees.

He immediately called me and told me she was one of the clients he always worried about and to make matters worse, he never had her sign any kind of investment policy statement. He invested her 90% in individual equities and 10% in cash and had zero documentation for his recommendations. Now this poor widow who knew very little about investments and made the biggest investment of her life just after her husband had died wanted to be reimbursed for her losses.

Things quickly got worse. It turns out that A. the seller didn't have any E&O insurance and that B. the plaintiff's attorney wasn't seeking $180,000 in lost damages. He was seeking over $500,000 based on the premise that she should receive not only what she lost (+ IA fees) but also what she could have made had he invested her in the S&P 500 index over what was now a 5-year period of time.

I spent the next few months periodically checking in with him as he hired his own securities attorney and tried to work out a settlement. The end he wrote her a check, out of pocket, for $90,000 (of which I am sure her attorney took 40%) and the matter was settled.

Case Study – Concentrated Stock Positions

By far one of the hardest things to deal with in this profession is concentrated stock positions.

More so than any other financial decision, a concentrated stock position has the potential to make or break a client's entire financial situation.

Let's say your client has stock in company XYZ and the position grows to a value of $5M. You could advise them to sell everything knowing the proceeds would be enough to meet all their goals. If you don't and the stock tanks, you are partially responsible (and wouldn't be a very good Advisor). At the same token, if the stock grows 10-fold after you told them to sell, they've missed a chance on creating generational wealth and it's "your fault".

There is probably no subject that in my career has been more incendiary than concentrated stock positions.

Let me illustrate with two real life examples:

In 2013 I met with a client that had $5M in Gilead stock. She was an executive assistant who started with the company near the very beginning and was awarded stock options which eventually converted to stock. She was making a salary of $60,000 per year and her husband, a former CPA, was unemployed. After building their financial plan, it was clear that they could sell all their stock, pay the taxes and retire. At the time the stock was around $110 a share. I suggested they do just that, and earmark anywhere from 1% - 3% of the proceeds to long-term call options. The theory being that if the stock tanked, they'd be happy they sold when they did and the money they "wasted" on the call options would act as a cheap insurance policy. The husband said, let's place a sell order at $120 per share. I pointed out to him that there was no guarantee that the stock would ever reach $120 a share and that it could easily get cut in half before reaching that price. That is exactly what the stock did. Gilead endured a series of negative outcomes from the FDA and the stock plummeted, falling to $60 a share, where it still stands almost a decade later. The client never sold their shares. I fired them as clients but my former colleague from my former firm kept in touch with them. She is still working, and her husband is still an out of work CPA.

Netflix Story – every lesson learned influences how you think about scenarios when you encounter them for the second time. Knowing this, in 2014 I met a prospective client who worked for Netflix, got paid in part via stock options with Netflix and invested a portion of his salary into Netflix stock via their employee stock participation plan. At the time, he was concerned that Netflix "might not make it" and asked what I thought he should do. I shared with him the story of the Gilead employee and admitted fully that my thinking when it came to concentrated stock positions was biased because of what I had experienced just a year earlier. This time however things played out quite differently. The client chose not to take my advice and allowed Netflix stock to remain 90%+ of his net worth. Over the ensuing 24+ months Netflix stock took off, and so did his net worth. He and his wife decided to fire me as their Advisor, even though they hadn't acted on my advice.

Now anyone who has read Annie Duke's work on "Thinking in Bets" knows that this is called "resulting" wherein you look at the result and not the thought process that went into it when examining the quality of a decision. In retrospect my advice to the Netflix engineer was good advice even though it would have produced a bad outcome had he taken it. I do think the lesson to be learned here is not that we should be able to predict which stocks will tank and which should flourish, but instead to share with clients, with full transparency, why we think the way we do and what biases influence our thinking. This is one of those times where we can only sit back at that point and let the client make the ultimate decision.

Case Study – An Annuity Sale Gone Wrong

In this story I was not the Advisor but rather I was managing the Advisor (at my previous firm) when this incident took place. An elderly client who had been sitting on cash asked the Advisor what she could do to earn a greater rate of return on her money. After doing a thorough review of her financial situation, the Advisor suggested she buy a fixed annuity that was paying a guaranteed interest rate of 5% per year for 5 years. This product had a steep penalty for early withdrawal. What makes this story particularly interesting is that the Advisor was the representative on the client's employer sponsored retirement plan, which happened to be a hospital 403b plan. As a result, the Advisor was at the hospital 1-2 times per month enrolling new employees into the hospital's retirement plan. If you've only worked in the 401K market this may seem foreign to you but in the 403b market which consists of hospitals, schools, and universities, having an on-site representative is not uncommon at all. Lo and behold the client has signed all the paperwork but she missed one signature. Fast forward a week or so and she is now a patient in the hospital that she works at. Thinking he is doing a good deed and going above and beyond, he visits her in the hospital and asks her to sign the form that she missed, which she gladly does.

Fast forward one year and her daughter asks her to borrow a substantial amount of money so she can make a down payment on a house. The client has no cash since she used it to buy this annuity. She calls the Advisor and says she wants to cancel her annuity and get her money back so she can help her daughter buy the house. The Advisor informs her that doing so will lead to a large surrender charge penalty, costing her thousands of dollars. She files a formal complaint against the Advisor, says she never understood that there was a surrender charge penalty for early withdrawal and that she was on pain medication and recovery from surgery when she signed the forms, so even though she acknowledged the surrender charges at the time, she was not of sound mind and body when doing so. We escalated all of this to our Chief Compliance Officer who heard the alarm bells ringing and said this was not going to end well for the Advisor, even though most of the paperwork was signed before she went in for surgery. An E&O claim was filed, the surrender charge penalty was paid by the E&O insurance provider (the Advisor paid his $5,000 deductible), and the client received her money back without penalty. This was the Advisor's first "complaint" in his 30 years as an Advisor and not one he could ever forget.

NOTES

NOTES

NOTES

NOTES

Made in the USA
Las Vegas, NV
04 January 2025

15904353R00098